W9-AHP-922

INTRODUCING
ISSUES WITH
OPPOSING
VIEWPOINTS®

Global Warming

Other books in the Introducing Issues
with Opposing Viewpoints series:

Advertising
AIDS
Alcohol
Animal Rights
Civil Liberties
Cloning
The Death Penalty
Drug Abuse
Drunk Driving
Energy Alternatives
The Environment
Euthanasia
Gangs
Gay Marriage
Genetic Engineering
Gun Control
Islam
Military Draft
Obesity
Pollution
Racism
Smoking
Teen Pregnancy
Terrorism
UFOs

INTRODUCING
ISSUES WITH
OPPOSING
VIEWPOINTS®

Global Warming

Dan Minkel, *Book Editor*

Christine Nasso, *Publisher*
Elizabeth Des Chenes, *Managing Editor*

GREENHAVEN PRESS
An imprint of Thomson Gale, a part of The Thomson Corporation

THOMSON
GALE

Detroit • New York • San Francisco • New Haven, Conn. • Waterville, Maine • London

For more information, contact
Greenhaven Press
27500 Drake Rd.
Farmington Hills, MI 48331-3535
Or you can visit our Internet site at http://www.gale.com

LIBRARY OF CONGRESS CATALOGING-IN-PUBLICATION DATA

Global warming / Dan Minkel, book editor.
    p. cm. - (Introducing issues with opposing viewpoints)
Includes bibliographical references and index.
ISBN-13: 978-0-7377-3564-2 (hardcover : alk. paper)
ISBN-10: 0-7377-3564-3 (hardcover : alk. paper)
1. Global warming. I. Minkel, Dan.
QC981.8.G56G5744 2006
363.738'74—dc22   2006030399

Printed in the United States of America

Contents

Foreword   7
Introduction   9

Chapter 1: How Serious Is the Problem of Global Warming?

1. Global Warming Is a Serious Problem   15
   David Wenban

2. Global Warming Is Not a Serious Problem   23
   James M. Inhofe

3. Humans Are Causing Global Warming   32
   Robert McCredie

4. Humans Are Not Causing Global Warming   38
   David Bellamy

5. Nuclear Power Will Help Reduce Global Warming   45
   Terry Wynn

6. Nuclear Power Will Not Help Reduce Global Warming   52
   M.V. Ramana

Chapter 2: What Problems Might Be Caused by Global Warming?

1. Global Warming Causes More Intense Hurricane Activity   59
   Derrick Z. Jackson

2. Global Warming Does Not Cause More Intense   65
   Hurricane Activity
   Charles C.W. Cooke and Alex Kormendi

3. Global Warming Will Raise Sea Levels   71
   Richard A. Kerr

4. Global Warming Will Lower Sea Levels   77
   World Climate Report

5. Global Warming Will Increase the World's Food Supply 82
   H. Sterling Burnett

6. Global Warming Will Decrease the World's Food Supply 88
   Martin Mittelstaedt

Facts About Global Warming 93
Glossary 95
Organizations to Contact 97
For Further Reading 102
Index 107
Picture Credits 111
About the Editor 112

Foreword

I ndulging in a wide spectrum of ideas, beliefs, and perspectives is a critical cornerstone of democracy. After all, it is often debates over differences of opinion, such as whether to legalize abortion, how to treat prisoners, or when to enact the death penalty, that shape our society and drive it forward. Such diversity of thought is frequently regarded as the hallmark of a healthy and civilized culture. As the Reverend Clifford Schutjer of the First Congregational Church in Mansfield, Ohio, declared in a 2001 sermon, "Surrounding oneself with only like-minded people, restricting what we listen to or read only to what we find agreeable is irresponsible. Refusing to entertain doubts once we make up our minds is a subtle but deadly form of arrogance." With this advice in mind, Introducing Issues with Opposing Viewpoints books aim to open readers' minds to the critically divergent views that comprise our world's most important debates.

Introducing Issues with Opposing Viewpoints simplifies for students the enormous and often overwhelming mass of material now available via print and electronic media. Collected in every volume is an array of opinions that captures the essence of a particular controversy or topic. Introducing Issues with Opposing Viewpoints books embody the spirit of nineteenth-century journalist Charles A. Dana's axiom: "Fight for your opinions, but do not believe that they contain the whole truth, or the only truth." Absorbing such contrasting opinions teaches students to analyze the strength of an argument and compare it to its opposition. From this process readers can inform and strengthen their own opinions, or be exposed to new information that will change their minds. Introducing Issues with Opposing Viewpoints is a mosaic of different voices. The authors are statesmen, pundits, academics, journalists, corporations, and ordinary people who have felt compelled to share their experiences and ideas in a public forum. Their words have been collected from newspapers, journals, books, speeches, interviews, and the Internet, the fastest growing body of opinionated material in the world.

Introducing Issues with Opposing Viewpoints shares many of the well-known features of its critically acclaimed parent series, Opposing Viewpoints. The articles are presented in a pro/con format, allowing readers to absorb divergent perspectives side by side. Active reading questions preface each viewpoint, requiring the student to approach the material thoughtfully and carefully. Useful charts, graphs, and cartoons supplement each article. A thorough introduction provides readers with crucial background on an issue. An annotated bibliography points the reader toward articles, books, and Web sites that contain additional information on the topic. An appendix of organizations to contact contains a wide variety of charities, nonprofit organizations, political groups, and private enterprises that each hold a position on the issue at hand. Finally, a comprehensive index allows readers to locate content quickly and efficiently.

Introducing Issues with Opposing Viewpoints is also significantly different from Opposing Viewpoints. As the series title implies, its presentation will help introduce students to the concept of opposing viewpoints, and learn to use this material to aid in critical writing and debate. The series' four-color, accessible format makes the books attractive and inviting to readers of all levels. In addition, each viewpoint has been carefully edited to maximize a reader's understanding of the content. Short but thorough viewpoints capture the essence of an argument. A substantial, thought-provoking essay question placed at the end of each viewpoint asks the student to further investigate the issues raised in the viewpoint, compare and contrast two authors' arguments, or consider how one might go about forming an opinion on the topic at hand. Each viewpoint contains sidebars that include at-a-glance information and handy statistics. A Facts About section located in the back of the book further supplies students with relevant facts and figures.

Following in the tradition of the Opposing Viewpoints series, Greenhaven Press continues to provide readers with invaluable exposure to the controversial issues that shape our world. As John Stuart Mill once wrote: "The only way in which a human being can make some approach to knowing the whole of a subject is by hearing what can be said about it by persons of every variety of opinion and studying all modes in which it can be looked at by every character of mind. No wise man ever acquired his wisdom in any mode but this." It is to this principle that Introducing Issues with Opposing Viewpoints books are dedicated.

Introduction

I n late August 2005 the U.S. Gulf Coast was preparing to be ripped to shreds by a massive hurricane brewing offshore. When Hurricane Katrina finally hit land on August 29, 2005, it made history as one of the largest hurricanes to hit the Gulf Coast region since 1969. Of all the towns and cities that were obliterated by Katrina, none was more publicized than the destruction of New Orleans. Though about 80 percent of the city had evacuated, more than one hundred thousand people remained to endure Katrina's 125-mile-per-hour winds and torrential rains. But the ravages of the storm were not the end of people's suffering; the storm caused levees

A woman surveys the damage caused by Hurricane Katrina, one of the deadliest storms ever to hit the United States.

at the perimeter of New Orleans to become swollen with water, which headed with ferocity toward the hurricane-battered city. About 80 percent of the city flooded, with some parts drowned under as much as twenty feet of water. The people who did not evacuate before the hurricane struck became prisoners in their homes. Some swam for their lives in the streets; others were trapped on the tiny islands of their attics or rooftops. When it was all over, Hurricane Katrina had killed more than eighteen hundred people across five states and left tens of thousands stranded, homeless, or even destitute. As of April 2006 Katrina's damages are estimated at $105 billion, making it the costliest natural disaster in U.S. history.

Before people had begun cleaning up the destruction—indeed, before many even made it back from refugee centers that had sprung up in the southern United States—policy makers, scientists, reporters, and officials began discussing whether the tremendous destruction they had witnessed had anything to do with global warming. The effects of global warming are thought to include frequent and violent natural disasters such as tornados, earthquakes—and hurricanes. As people looked upon the ruins of New Orleans and hundreds of other towns along the coast, many thought to themselves: Is it here? Is this the apocalyptic global warming that scientists have warned about?

Increasing hurricane activity is part of many global warming models. Some scientists believe that global warming causes the oceans' temperatures to rise, which can increase the frequency and strength of hurricanes as they gather over water. The United States has certainly experienced more frequent and violent hurricanes in recent decades. One hurricane wake-up call came in 1992 when Hurricane Andrew ripped through Florida, causing $39 billion worth of damage. In fact, Andrew was the most damaging hurricane in U.S. history until Katrina struck. Following Andrew, a record thirty-three hurricanes struck the Atlantic basin from 1995 to 1999. Other countries have also experienced increasing storm activity: In 2004, for example, Japan set an all-time record for typhoons. For people such as former vice president Al Gore, Katrina and other intensifying weather patterns are clear proof that global warming is here. As he said in a September 2005 speech about the link between global warming and Katrina, "The scientific community is warning us that

Former vice president Al Gore gives a presentation on global warming. Gore believes global warming is a serious threat to humanity.

the average hurricane will continue to get stronger because of global warming. . . . And the pattern is exactly consistent with what scientists have predicted for twenty years." Gore and others urge the global community to use tragedies like Katrina to take action against further damage from natural disasters. Says writer Derrick Z. Jackson, "The one-two punch of Katrina and Rita [a hurricane that followed Katrina] does not yet have us reaching for the smelling salts. We are still waiting for global warming to hit us below the belt."

But opponents of the theory that global warming is to blame for increasingly violent weather point out that in some places where hurricanes occur—places such as the northern Indian Ocean and regions near Australia—the frequency of hurricanes has actually dropped. Furthermore, researchers such as hurricane scientist William Gray point out that hurricane seasons are cyclical—they grow weaker and stronger over twenty- to forty-year periods. In fact, the last period of high hurricane activity took place between the 1920s and 1960s—a period too early to have been affected by man-made global warming. Authors Alex Kormendi and Charles C.W. Cooke write, "Given that patterns in hurricanes seem driven by 20–40 year cycles, to draw solid conclusions from a period that began in the 1970s and neglect prior natural patterns is a bit like staying up from 5 A.M. to 9 A.M. and finding there is a trend that the Earth is getting brighter."

Furthermore, some analysts argue that record-breaking amounts of property damage caused by hurricanes is less due to any growing intensity of storms and more to increased population booms in hurricane-prone areas. For example, Miami—a city that lies in the path of many storms—underwent a forty-two-year period without getting struck by an intense hurricane. In that time Miami's population grew by more than 600 percent, with developers building houses and other expensive infrastructure to support the growing population. When Hurricane Andrew struck in 1992, therefore, rates of property damage were outrageously high because so many people had settled in the region. According to Christopher Landsea of the National Oceanic and Atmospheric Administration (NOAA), a "large portion of [the] immense toll [of high-profile hurricanes] is due to the property development and population increases along the U.S. coastal states."

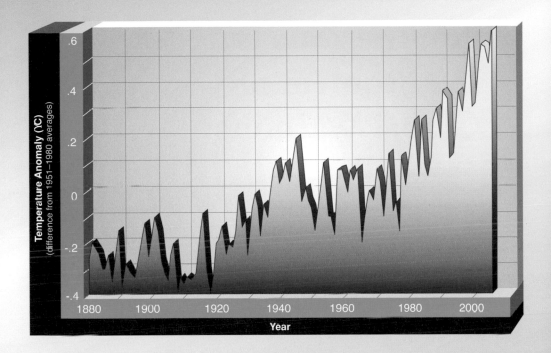

Source: NASA/Goddard Institute for Space Studies (http://data.giss.nasa.gov), 2006.

Whether or not global warming is causing fierce storms like Hurricane Katrina will continue to be a point of discussion among scientists, policy makers, and others throughout the twenty-first century. This and other debates are presented in *Introducing Issues with Opposing Viewpoints: Global Warming.* Readers will be exposed to varying opinions on the seriousness of global warming, what problems might be caused by global warming, and how global warming might be slowed or reversed.

Chapter 1

How Serious Is the Problem of Global Warming?

Scientists measure the thickness of a glacier. Melting glaciers could indicate global warming.

Global Warming Is a Serious Problem

"The world is undergoing the greatest change in temperature since the last ice age."

David Wenban

In the following viewpoint author David Wenban argues that global warming is the most critical problem facing humanity. He explains that global warming is caused by man-made greenhouse gases resulting from the burning of fossil fuels such as coal and oil. Global warming could lead to a host of weather-related problems such as the recent hurricane in New Orleans, he warns. Wenban concludes that immediate action is needed to prevent such disasters.

AS YOU READ, CONSIDER THE FOLLOWING QUESTIONS:

1. According to Wenban, what would happen to shellfish and coral if the oceans become more acidic?
2. According to the International Climate Change Task Force, when will the tipping points on climate change be reached?
3. According to climatologist James Lovelock, what would be the result of a two-degree rise in atmospheric temperature?

T he world faces enormous changes in weather patterns and other natural phenomena. These changes have resulted from the emission of man-made pollutants from traditional, non-renewable fuels such as coal and oil in energy production. . . .

Unless strong and decisive political action is taken to halt greenhouse gas emissions, these changes will cause rising sea levels, and a general rise in world temperatures, with extreme heat variations, as well as drought, floods, hurricanes, cyclones, and carbon dioxide pollution on a global scale. Many species of animals, birds, aquatic and plant life will perish. There will be mass loss of human life, the spread or exacerbation of diseases, dislocation of entire populations, geopolitical instability and a disastrous decrease in the quality of human life.

Tipping Points

Unless we act, these changes may well happen within the lifetime of today's children. Critical factors are the "tipping points" (i.e. the times when various adverse changes become virtually inevitable). The International Climate Change Task Force (ICCTF) says that these points could be reached by 2100. However, other authorities consider that some could be reached in 15 to 20 years' time.

Over the last two decades the more optimistic predictions of conservative scientific organisations such as the ICCTF have had to be revised. The average world temperature for 2058, which it predicted several years ago, was actually reached last year! Unless realistic measures are taken to reverse the rapid rise of the temperature of the earth's atmosphere, the "tipping points" will arrive sooner than later.

Threatening Weather Trends

Serious atmospheric pollution began during the industrial revolution. For about 400,000 years the atmosphere's carbon dioxide level remained the same, but it's now rapidly rising.

This is causing two specific weather trends. The depletion of rainforests and the increasing use of fossil fuels have increased the emission of greenhouse gases (mainly CO_2 and five other gases) that trap solar radiation within the atmosphere, gradually increasing temperatures worldwide. At the same time carbon dioxide lodged within clouds deflects solar radiation ("global dimming"). This reduces evaporation from oceans and lakes, leading to prolonged droughts.

Coal-burning power plants release large amounts of carbon dioxide into the atmosphere, which could be a cause of global warming.

Parts of the Amazon Jungle (the "lungs of the world") are being cleared for short-term profit and provision of land for settlement. Climatologist James Lovelock has predicted that a two-degree atmospheric temperature rise would cause the jungle to die, and to become an emitter of carbon dioxide rather than oxygen. Breathing the earth's atmosphere would presumably become increasingly difficult. As a result of global warming fires in many countries are becoming more frequent and severe and cause major damage and pollution. The increase in droughts, hurricanes, floods and extreme weather conditions has recently caused a 500 percent increase in natural catastrophes, according to one French insurance company.

Temperatures Are Changing Fast

The world is undergoing the greatest change in temperature since the last ice age, and the change is happening faster than ever before. Forty percent of Alaska's ice coverage has disappeared in recent times.

The Greenhouse Effect

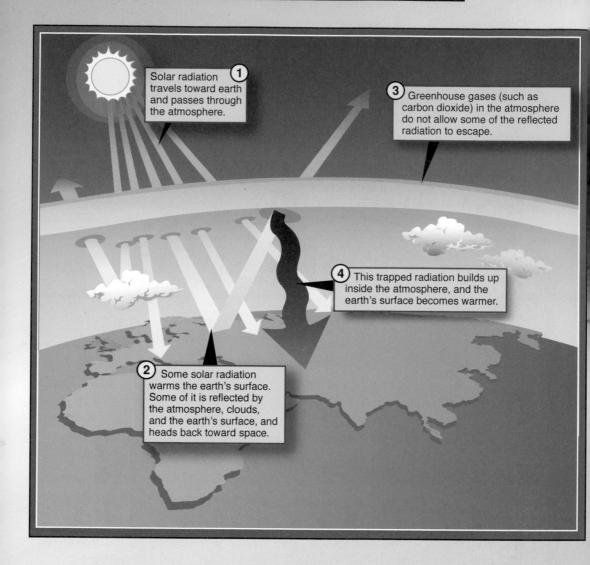

1 Solar radiation travels toward earth and passes through the atmosphere.

3 Greenhouse gases (such as carbon dioxide) in the atmosphere do not allow some of the reflected radiation to escape.

4 This trapped radiation builds up inside the atmosphere, and the earth's surface becomes warmer.

2 Some solar radiation warms the earth's surface. Some of it is reflected by the atmosphere, clouds, and the earth's surface, and heads back toward space.

In 2001, Australian scientists found that Heard Island glaciers had shrunk by one third in the past 50 years. [In 2004] scientists discovered that the polar ice was melting nine times faster than it had been in 1994.

If the world's major ice shelves melted, which could happen by the end of this century or even sooner, the oceans would rise by 7–14 metres, according to Lovelock. The initial rise would occur quickly after the polar ice began to break up, according to Australian Antarctic scientists.

The recent devastation of New Orleans [due to Hurricane Katrina in 2005] has given a miniscule indication of the impact on the world's coastal populations. Melting of the polar caps would flood low-lying countries such as the Netherlands and Bangladesh. This could include Calcutta with 16 million people and scores of other coastal cities and towns are at risk. More than a billion people would die, mostly in the world's poorer countries. Whole Pacific islands could disappear under water. Australia's wonderful beaches would disappear, and the Great Barrier Reef would have died long before this.

Oceans Are Becoming Acidic

Fossil fuel emissions, which dissolve in sea water to form hydrogen ions, have made sea water more acidic than for millions of years. The oceans have soaked up the CO_2 emitted over the last 200 years, and they are now absorbing a tonne of CO_2 per capita every year. But they may be reaching saturation point.

Tropical reefs may cease to provide protection from destructive waves by 2050. Shellfish and coral will have difficulty forming and maintaining their shells and skeletons because of the higher acidity. By 2010, acidic seas could also limit plankton growth. The supply of sea food for humans could decline, and the sea's lessened ability to absorb CO_2 will accelerate climate change. . . .

Different Options for Avoiding Disaster

The world's greenhouse gas emissions must be reduced, and the world's forested areas must be protected. To avoid a "tipping point" temperature rise (at 3.6 degrees higher than in pre-industrial times), we must keep the atmospheric carbon dioxide below 440 parts per million (ppm). It's already at 370 ppm, and rising.

The Kyoto Protocol requires a reduction of five percent in emissions compared with 1990 levels by 2012, but scientists say that between 60 and 80 percent is needed.

There have been many proposals for the best way to achieve this. . . .

Some scientists have advocated a reduction in energy consumption, so that worldwide carbon production does not exceed 2.5 tonnes of carbon per capita per annum. In order to achieve this, the

The Perito Moreno glacier, located in Argentina, dramatically ruptures. Unstable glaciers could melt, causing sea levels to rise dangerously.

rate of CO_2 production per kilometre of travel, and the level of vehicle use, would both have to be cut. Any move to implement this would be vigorously opposed by the vehicle industry. . . .

Some experts believe that natural gas should be used for energy production, and that energy production from alternative sources should be raised sharply.

Some business groups and politicians have advocated building nuclear power stations, despite the possibility of catastrophic accidents, and the danger and huge cost of storing nuclear waste. They have pointed out that nuclear energy produces no carbon emissions. Despite the example of Chernobyl, they also claim that the number of deaths from nuclear accidents has been small, compared to the casualties from wars, motor accidents, and fossil fuel pollution.

Because of the growing urgency of the global warming threat, some scientists have reluctantly come to agree with them. However, others have objected that construction of nuclear power stations would in itself take decades, requiring long term waste storage at enormous cost, and could result in accidents, threatening the lives and health of hundreds of thousands of people.

Environmentalists believe that using clean, renewable resources such as wind power could stave off global warming.

They favour wind, solar, hydroelectric power and other under-utilised alternative means of energy production. Some countries have already constructed wind power stations, despite problems in maintaining a stable energy supply, and other problems, such as objections to the visual impact of wind turbines. . . .

Global Warming Is Undeniable

Combating global warming would involve taking forceful steps to reduce pollution, and is therefore vigorously opposed by certain sections of capital.

These interest groups have recruited a small number of scientists who claim that there's really nothing to worry about, even though most of the world's scientists say unequivocally that global warming is undeniable, and that we need to tackle it immediately and vigorously.

EVALUATING THE AUTHORS' ARGUMENTS:

In the viewpoint you just read, the author used weather forecasts to argue global warming is a serious problem. The author of the next viewpoint uses weather forecasts to argue that global warming is not a serious problem. In your opinion, which author is more convincing? After reading both viewpoints, do you believe that global warming is a serious problem or not?

Global Warming Is Not a Serious Problem

James M. Inhofe

"Much of the debate over global warming is predicated on fear, rather than science."

The following viewpoint is taken from a speech given on the Senate floor by Senator James M. Inhofe of Oklahoma. Inhofe believes that global warming is an unproven theory being pushed by alarmists. He uses climate records to refute the allegations that global warming is a manmade phenomenon. He also argues that global warming would not bring terrible, catastrophic conditions but instead would benefit humanity. Americans must avoid buying into fear tactics and fraudulent science, he concludes.

Inhofe is the chairman of the Committee on Environment and Public Works.

AS YOU READ, CONSIDER THE FOLLOWING QUESTIONS:

1. What is the troposphere, as described by Inhofe?
2. What evidence led Inhofe to conclude that the warming trend of the early twentieth century was caused by natural factors?

James M. Inhofe, "The Science of Climate Change," Senate floor statement, July 28, 2003.

M uch of the debate over global warming is predicated on fear, rather than science. Global warming alarmists see a future plagued by catastrophic flooding, war, terrorism, economic dislocations, droughts, crop failures, mosquito-borne diseases, and harsh weather—all caused by man-made greenhouse gas emissions. . . .

Refuting Global Warming

Today, even saying there is scientific disagreement over global warming is itself controversial. But anyone who pays even cursory attention to the issue understands that scientists vigorously disagree over whether human activities are responsible for global warming, or whether those activities will precipitate natural disasters.

I would submit, furthermore, that not only is there a debate, but the debate is shifting away from those who subscribe to global warming alarmism. After studying the issue over the last several years,

I believe that the balance of the evidence offers strong proof that natural variability is the overwhelming factor influencing climate.

It's also important to question whether global warming is even a problem for human existence. Thus far no one has seriously demonstrated any scientific proof that increased global temperatures would

lead to the catastrophes predicted by alarmists. In fact, it appears that just the opposite is true: that increases in global temperatures may have a beneficial effect on how we live our lives.

For these reasons I would like to discuss an important body of scientific research that refutes the anthropogenic [caused by man] theory of catastrophic global warming. I believe this research offers compelling proof that human activities have little impact on climate. . . .

No Meaningful Warming Trend

[Let's examine] temperature trends in the 20th century. GCMs [global climate models] predict that rising atmospheric CO_2 concentrations will cause temperatures in the troposphere, the layer from 5,000 to 30,000 feet, to rise faster than surface temperatures—a critical fact supporting the alarmist hypothesis.

But in fact, there is no meaningful warming trend in the troposphere, and weather satellites, widely considered the most accurate measure of global temperatures, have confirmed this.

To illustrate this point, just think about a greenhouse. The glass panes let sunlight in but prevent it from escaping. The greenhouse then warms from the top down. As is clear from the science, this simply is not happening in the atmosphere.

Satellite measurements are validated independently by measurements from NOAA [National Oceanic and Atmospheric Administration] balloon radiosonde instruments, whose records extend back over 40 years.

If you look at this chart of balloon data extremists will tell you that warming is occurring, but if you look more closely you see that temperature in 1955 was higher than temperature in 2000.

A weather balloon with radiosonde instruments is released to collect data about the atmosphere. Such measurements have not showed any meaningful warming trend.

A recent detailed comparison of atmospheric temperature data gathered by satellites with widely-used data gathered by weather balloons corroborates both the accuracy of the satellite data and the rate of global warming seen in that data.

Using NOAA satellite readings of temperatures in the lower atmosphere, scientists at The University of Alabama in Huntsville (UAH) produced a dataset that shows global atmospheric warming at the rate of about 0.07 degrees C (about 0.13 degrees Fahrenheit) per decade since November 1978.

"That works out to a global warming trend of about one and a quarter degrees Fahrenheit over 100 years," said Dr. John Christy, who compiled the comparison data. Christy concedes that such a trend "is probably due in part to human influences," but adds that "it's substantially less than the warming forecast by most climate models, and"—here is the key point—"it isn't entirely out of the range of climate change we might expect from natural causes."

To reiterate: the best data collected from satellites validated by balloons to test the hypothesis of a human-induced global warming from the release of CO_2 into the atmosphere show no meaningful trend of increasing temperatures, even as the climate models exaggerated the warmth that ought to have occurred from a build-up in CO_2. . . .

No Support for Man-Made Warming

When we look at the 20th century as a whole, we see some distinct phases that question anthropogenic theories of global warming. First, a strong warming trend of about 0.5 degrees C began in the late 19th century and peaked around 1940. Next, the temperature decreased from 1940 until the late 1970s.

Why is that decrease significant? Because about 80% of the carbon dioxide from human activities was added to the air after 1940, meaning the early 20th century warming trend had to be largely natural.

Scientists from the Scripps Institution of Oceanography confirmed this phenomenon in the March 12, 1999 issue of the journal *Science*. They addressed the proverbial "chicken-and-egg" question of climate science, namely: when the Earth shifts from glacial to warm periods, which comes first: an increase in atmospheric carbon dioxide levels, or an increase in global temperature?

The team concluded that the temperature rise comes first, followed by a carbon dioxide boost 400 to 1,000 years later. This contradicts everything alarmists have been saying about man-made global warming in the 20th century. . . .

Is Global Warming Bad?

Even as we discuss whether temperatures will go up or down, we should ask whether global warming would actually produce the catastrophic effects its adherents so confidently predict.

What gets obscured in the global warming debate is the fact that carbon dioxide is not a pollutant. It is necessary for life. Numerous studies have shown that global warming can actually be beneficial to mankind.

Most plants, especially wheat and rice, grow considerably better when there is more CO_2 in the atmosphere. CO_2 works like a fertilizer and higher temperatures usually further enhance the CO_2 fertilizer effect.

In fact the average crop, according to Dr. John Reilly, of the MIT Joint Program on the Science and Policy of Global Change, is 30 percent higher in a CO_2-enhanced world. I want to repeat that: PRODUCTIVITY IS 30 PERCENT HIGHER IN A CO_2-ENHANCED WORLD. This is not just a matter of opinion, but a well-established phenomenon.

With regard to the impact of global warming on human health, it is assumed that higher temperatures will induce more deaths and massive outbreaks of deadly diseases. In particular, a frequent scare tactic by alarmists is that warmer temperatures will spark malaria outbreaks. Dr. Paul Reiter convincingly debunks this claim in a 2000 study for the Centers for Disease Control. As Reiter found, "Until the second half of the 20th century, malaria was endemic and widespread in many temperate regions,"—this next point is critical—"with major epidemics as far north as the Arctic Circle."

Reiter also published a second study in the March 2001 issue of *Environmental Health Perspectives* showing that "despite spectacular cooling [of the Little Ice Age], malaria persisted throughout Europe."

Another myth is that warming increases morbidity rates. This isn't the case, according to Dr. Robert Mendelsohn, an environmental economist from Yale University. Mendelsohn argues that heat-stress

Greenhouse Gases and Climate Change Through the Ages

By analyzing many miles-deep ice-core samples, scientists can estimate surface temperatures and atmospheric gases that existed many thousands of years ago. These ice-core results show a definite relationship between greenhouse gases (carbon dioxide and methane) and temperatures, although some scientists still question whether more gases trigger higher temperatures, or the other way around.

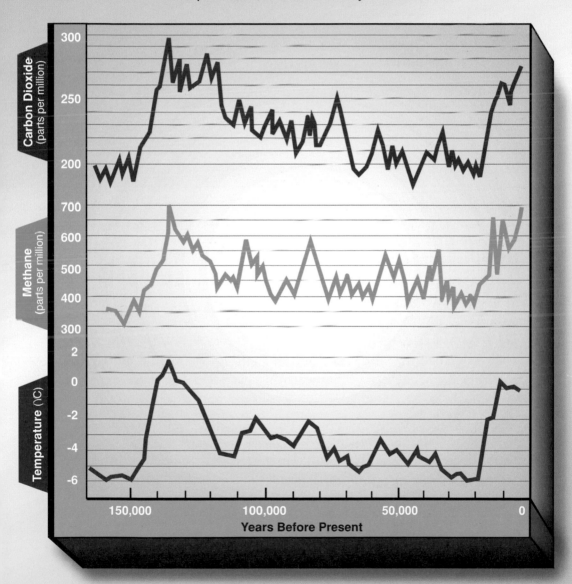

Source: National Climatic Data Center/National Oceanic and Atmospheric Administration (www.ncdc.noaa.gov), 1998.

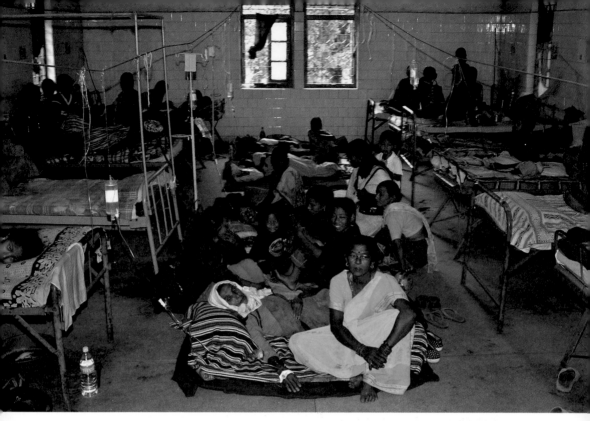

Malaria sufferers wait for treatment in a clinic in India. Some experts refute claims that global warming could cause a malaria outbreak.

deaths are caused by temperature variability and not warming. Those deaths grow in number not as climates warm but as the variability in climate increases. . . .

Global Warming Is Not a Fact

I am mystified that some in this body, and in the media, blithely assert that the science of global warming is settled—that is, fossil fuel emissions are the principal, driving cause of global warming. In a recent letter to me concerning the next EPA administrator, two senators wrote that "the pressing problem of global warming" is now an "established scientific fact," and demanded that the new administrator commit to addressing it.

With all due respect, this statement is baseless, for several reasons. As I outlined in detail above, the evidence is overwhelmingly in favor of those who don't see global warming posing grave harm to the planet and who don't think human beings have significant influence on the climate system. . . .

It is my fervent hope that Congress will reject prophets of doom who peddle propaganda masquerading as science in the name of saving the planet from catastrophic disaster. I urge my colleagues to put stock in scientists who rely on the best, most objective scientific data and reject fear as a motivating basis for making public policy decisions.

EVALUATING THE AUTHORS' ARGUMENTS:

In the viewpoint you just read, the author calls those who disagree with him "alarmists," "prophets of doom," and peddlers of "propaganda." How do these descriptions affect the way you think of the issues at hand? Does this technique increase the effectiveness of the author's arguments? Why or why not?

Humans Are Causing Global Warming

Robert McCredie

"Climate change is undeniably real, caused by human activities, and has serious consequences."

In the following viewpoint Robert Mc-Credie, Lord May of Oxford, argues that human activity has caused global warming by raising the levels of carbon dioxide in the atmosphere. Prior to the Industrial Revolution, he claims, carbon dioxide levels had been relatively constant. But since that time, they have been rising at an ever-increasing rate. McCredie warns that global warming will continue to worsen unless humans curb the industrial activities that contribute to the problem.

AS YOU READ, CONSIDER THE FOLLOWING QUESTIONS:

1. As described by McCredie, what are some of the impacts of global warming?
2. When did the Industrial Revolution begin, as reported by the author?
3. What are some ways in which humans could reverse global warming, according to McCredie?

The Industrial Revolution may be said to have begun in the 1780s, after James Watt developed his steam engine. At this time, ice-core records show that levels of carbon dioxide in

Robert McCredie, Lord May of Oxford, Annual Anniversary Address to the Royal Society, November 30, 2005. Reproduced by permission.

the atmosphere were around 280 parts per million (ppm). Give or take 10 ppm, this had been their level for the past 6,000 years, since the beginning of the first cities. . . .

Carbon Dioxide Levels Rose with Industrialization

After the 1780s, as industrialization drove up the burning up of fossil fuels in the developed world, carbon dioxide levels rose. At first the rise was slow. It took about a century and a half to reach 315 ppm. Accelerating during the 20th century, levels reached 330 ppm by the mid-1970s; 360 ppm by the 1990s; 380 ppm today.

This change of magnitude by 20 ppm over only a decade has not been seen since the most recent ice age ended, ushering in the dawn of the Holocene epoch, around 10,000 years ago. And if current trends continue, by about 2050 atmospheric carbon dioxide levels will have reached more than 500 ppm, nearly double pre-industrial levels. . . .

A scientist handles ice core samples in a freezer. Ice core samples reveal a glacier's history and are used to investigate whether ice caps are changing shape.

Projected Global Temperature Increase

Using climate models based on rising carbon dioxide levels, the Intergovernmental Panel on Climate Change estimates that average global temperatures will rise between 2.5℉ and 10.5℉ (1.4℃ and 5.8℃) by the year 2100, compared with the average global temperature in 1990.

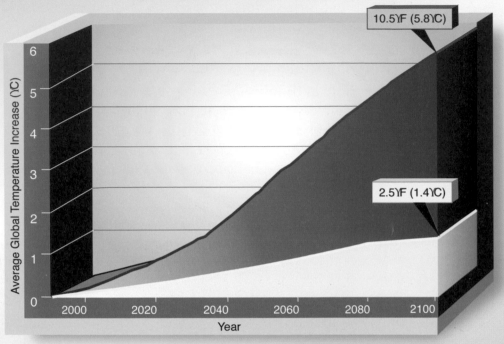

Source: Intergovernmental Panel on Climate Change (www.ipcc.ch), Third Assessment Report, 2001.

Such increases in the concentrations of the greenhouse gases which blanket our planet will cause global warming. . . . In their most recent report in 2001, the Intergovernmental Panel on Climate Change (IPCC) concluded that this warming would be in the range of 1.4 to 5.8 degrees Celsius by 2100. This would be the warmest period on Earth for at least the last 100,000 years.

Global Warming Will Be Catastrophic

Many people—especially, it would seem, some economists—find it hard to grasp the significance of such a seemingly small change, given that temperatures can differ from one day to the next by 100 degrees Celsius. There is a huge difference between daily fluctuations, and global averages sustained year on year; the difference in average global temperature between today and the last ice age is only around five degrees Celsius.

The impacts of global warming are many and serious: sea level rise as mentioned above—which comes both from warmer water expanding, and also from ice melting at the poles; changes in availability of fresh water in a world where human numbers already press hard on available supplies in many countries; and the increasing incidence of extreme events—floods, droughts, and hurricanes—the serious consequences of which are rising to levels which invite comparison with "weapons of mass destruction.". . .

Floating houses such as this one are constructed in the Netherlands as a precaution against a dramatic rise in sea levels.

Actions We Must Take

So what should we be doing? One thing is very clear. The magnitude of the problem we face is such that there is no single answer, but rather a wide range of actions must be pursued. Broadly, I think these can be divided into four categories.

First, we can adapt to change: stop building on flood plains; start thinking more deliberately about coastal defences and flood protection, recognizing that some areas should, in effect, be given up. In Holland, one quarter of which lies below sea-level, there are already plans for houses designed to float on seasonally flooded areas.

Second, we can reduce inputs of carbon dioxide by reducing wasteful energy consumption. There are studies, for example, both in the US and in the UK, which demonstrate we can design housing which consumes roughly half current energy levels without significantly reducing living standards.

Third, we could capture some of the carbon dioxide emitted in burning fossil fuels, at the source, and sequester it—burying it on land or under the seabed.

Fourth, we could move toward renewable sources of energy, which do not put greenhouse gases into the atmosphere. These include geothermal, wind, wave, and water energy; solar energy from physics-based or biology-based devices; fission, currently generating seven percent of all the world's energy, and—despite its problems—surely playing a necessary role in the medium-term; fusion, a realistic long-term possibility; biomass—assuming that the carbon dioxide you put into the atmosphere was carbon dioxide you took out when you grew the fuel. . . .

The Human Effect on Climate Change

Not surprisingly, there exists a climate change "denial lobby," funded to the tune of tens of millions of dollars by sectors of the hydrocarbon industry, and highly influential in some countries. This lobby has understandable similarities, in attitudes and tactics, to the tobacco lobby that continues to deny smoking causes lung cancer, or the curious lobby denying that HIV causes AIDS.

Earlier, when some aspects of the science were less well understood, they denied the existence of evidence that human inputs of carbon dioxide and other greenhouse gases were causing global warming. More recently, there is acknowledgement of anthropogenic climate change, albeit expressed evasively, but accompanied by arguments that the effects are relatively insignificant, and/or that we should wait and see, and/or that technology will fix it anyway.

But make no mistake, climate change is undeniably real, caused by human activities, and has serious consequences.

EVALUATING THE AUTHORS' ARGUMENTS:

The author of this viewpoint argues that the recent warm weather trend results from human activities that have put more carbon dioxide in the atmosphere. The next viewpoint argues that the recent warm weather trend is natural rather than man-made. Which viewpoint do you find more persuasive, and why? Explain your answer.

Humans Are Not Causing Global Warming

David Bellamy

"The link between the burning of fossil fuels and global warming is a myth."

Global warming is a natural phenomenon not caused by human activity, according to David Bellamy in the following viewpoint. He points out that the earth has had a long history of warming and cooling trends. This cycle has several natural explanations, he explains, that have to do with the tilt of Earth's axis. Bellamy rejects the idea that the burning of fossil fuels is the cause of global warming and urges people to not waste their time and money on proposed global warming solutions that target human activity.

Bellamy is the author of over forty books and over eighty scientific papers relating to ecology and the environment.

AS YOU READ, CONSIDER THE FOLLOWING QUESTIONS:

1. What does the author say is to blame for rising sea levels in southern England?

2. According to Bellamy, what is the main greenhouse gas?

3. What are Milankovitch cycles, as described by the author?

Global warming—at least the modern nightmare version—is a myth. I am sure of it and so are a growing number of scientists. But what is really worrying is that the world's politicians and policy makers are not.

Human Activity Is Not the Problem

Instead, they have an unshakeable [belief] in what has, unfortunately, become one of the central credos of the environmental movement. Humans burn fossil fuels, which release increased levels of carbon dioxide—the principal so-called greenhouse gas—into the atmosphere, causing the atmosphere to heat up.

Andy Singer. © Andy Singer; www.andysinger.com. Reproduced by permission.

They say this is global warming: I say this is poppycock. Unfortunately, for the time being, it is their view that prevails.

As a result of their ignorance, the world's economy may be about to divert billions, nay trillions of pounds, dollars and roubles into solving a problem that actually doesn't exist. The waste of economic resources is incalculable and tragic.

To explain why I believe that global warming is largely a natural phenomenon that has been with us for 13,000 years and probably isn't causing us any harm anyway, we need to take heed of some basic facts of botanical science.

Carbon Dioxide Is Good

For a start, carbon dioxide is *not* the dreaded killer greenhouse gas that the 1992 Earth Summit in Rio de Janeiro and the subsequent

World leaders meet at the Kyoto Symposium in 2005 to discuss the Kyoto Protocol, a controversial treaty that deals with reducing global warming.

Kyoto Protocol five years later cracked it up to be. It is, in fact, the most important airborne fertiliser in the world, and without it there would be no green plants at all.

That is because, as any schoolchild will tell you, plants take in carbon dioxide and water and, with the help of a little sunshine, convert them into complex carbon compounds—that we either eat, build with or just admire—and oxygen, which just happens to keep the rest of the planet alive.

Increase the amount of carbon dioxide in the atmosphere, double it even, and this would produce a rise in plant productivity. Call me a biased old plant lover but that doesn't sound like much of a killer gas to me. Hooray for global warming is what I say, and so do a lot of my fellow scientists.

Let me quote from a petition produced by the Oregon Institute of Science and Medicine, which has been signed by over 18,000 scientists who are totally opposed to the Kyoto Protocol, which committed the world's leading industrial nations to cut their production of greenhouse gasses from fossil fuels.

They say: 'Predictions of harmful climatic effects due to future increases in minor greenhouse gasses like carbon dioxide are in error and do not conform to experimental knowledge.'

Global Warming Is Not to Blame

You couldn't get much plainer than that. And yet we still have public figures such as Sir David King, scientific adviser to Her Majesty's Government [Britain], making preposterous statements such as 'by the end of this century, the only continent we will be able to live on is Antarctica.'

At the same time, he's joined the bandwagon that blames just about everything on global warming, regardless of the scientific evidence. For example, take the alarm about rising sea levels around the south coast of England and subsequent flooding along the region's rivers. According to Sir David, global warming is largely to blame.

But it isn't at all—it's down to bad management of water catchments, building on flood plains and the incontestable fact that the south of England is gradually sinking below the waves.

And that sinking is nothing to do with rising sea levels caused by ice-caps melting. Instead, it is purely related to an entirely natural warping of the Earth's crust, which could only be reversed by sticking one of the enormously heavy ice-caps from past ice ages back on top of Scotland.

Natural Cycles of Warming and Cooling

Ah, ice ages . . . those absolutely massive changes in global climate that environmentalists don't like to talk about because they provide such strong evidence that climate change is an entirely natural phenomenon.

It was round about the end of the last ice age, some 13,000 years ago, that a global warming process did undoubtedly begin.

Not because of all those Stone age folk roasting mammoth meat on fossil fuel camp fires but because of something called the 'Milankovitch Cycles,' an entirely natural fact of planetary life that depends on the tilt of the Earth's axis and its orbit around the sun.

The glaciers melted, the ice cap retreated and Stone Age man could begin hunting again. But a couple of millennia later, it got very cold again and everyone headed south. Then it warmed up so much that water from melted ice filled the English Channel and [Britain] became an island.

The truth is that the climate has been yo-yo-ing up and down ever since. Whereas it was warm enough for Romans to produce good wine in York [in England around A.D. 80], on the other hand, [in about A.D. 1030] King Canute had to dig up peat to warm his people. And then it started getting warm again.

Up and down, up and down—that is how temperature and climate have always gone in the past and there is no proof they are not still doing exactly the same thing now. In other words, climate change is an entirely natural phenomenon, nothing to do with the burning of fossil fuels. . . .

Humans Have Nothing to Do with It

The real truth is that the main greenhouse gas—the one that has the most direct effect on land temperature—is water vapour, 99 per cent of which is entirely natural.

If all the water vapour was removed from the atmosphere, the temperature would fall by 33 degrees Celsius. But, remove all the carbon dioxide and the temperature might fall by just 0.3 per cent.

How Earth's Tilt Could Affect Climate

Serbian astronomer Milutin Milankovitch calculated changes in Earth's orbit, tilt, and wobble, all of which gradually change over the course of many thousands of years. These factors could affect climate because they all influence how much of the sun's radiation hits Earth's surface.

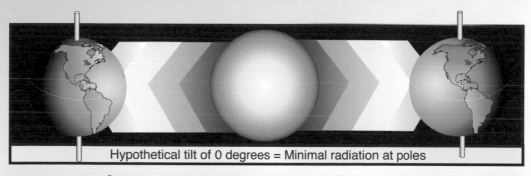

Hypothetical tilt of 0 degrees = Minimal radiation at poles

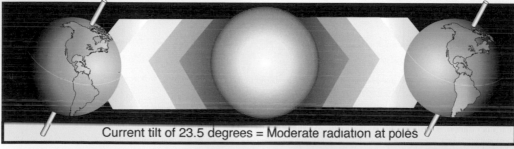

Current tilt of 23.5 degrees = Moderate radiation at poles

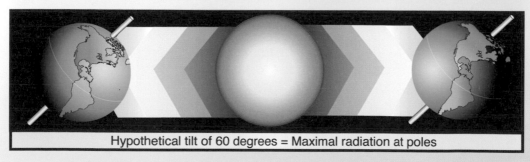

Hypothetical tilt of 60 degrees = Maximal radiation at poles

The tilt of Earth's axis varies between 22.1 and 24.5 degrees over a cycle of 40,000 years.

Source: National Climatic Data Center/NOAA (www.ncdc.noaa.gov).

Although we wouldn't be around, because without it there would be no green plants, no herbivorous farm animals and no food for us to eat. . . .

The link between the burning of fossil fuels and global warming is a myth. It is time the world's leaders, their scientific advisers and many environmental pressure groups woke up to the fact.

EVALUATING THE AUTHORS' ARGUMENTS:

In the viewpoint you just read, Bellamy uses historical events to argue that human activities are not responsible for global warming. What are these historical events? After reading about them, do you agree with Bellamy that global warming is a natural phenomenon?

Viewpoint

5

Nuclear Power Will Help Reduce Global Warming

"The life cycle of a nuclear power plant, from conception to decommissioning, emits almost no CO_2 to the atmosphere."

Terry Wynn

Using nuclear energy is the only practical way to reduce global warming, according to the author of the following viewpoint. Terry Wynn claims that nuclear power is the only energy source that can supply a significant share of the world's power needs without adding to the carbon dioxide emissions that cause global warming. Wynn says that other zero-emission forms of energy, such as wind, solar, and hydropower, either cause other environmental problems or are incapable of generating the quantity of power needed. He concludes that nuclear power is a safe and affordable power source that should be pursued to reduce global warming.

Wynn has been a member of the European Parliament since 1989.

AS YOU READ, CONSIDER THE FOLLOWING QUESTIONS:

1. What is the author's concern with power sources such as gas, oil, and coal?

Terry Wynn, "Nuclear Energy: Real Power, Real Solutions," *The Parliament Magazine*, October 17, 2005.
© TheParliament.com. Reproduced by permission.

2. According to Wynn, how many megawatts (MW) would a wind farm need to output in order to deliver the same power as a 1600 MW nuclear power plant?

3. What is the author's opinion on the usefulness of hydrogen cells?

First, lets get real about climate change. I've been an MEP [member of the European Parliament] almost since Adam was a lad, and in that time, the notion that climate change is both real and a serious threat to the lives of our children, grandchildren and beyond—if there is a 'beyond'—has become generally accepted. Now, let's get real too, about what can be done to ensure that future generations will survive with a quality of life akin to ours. I'm not naturally a pessimist but, quite frankly, a lot of what I hear on this subject fills me with doubt—unless I put it all together alongside the maintenance of today's nuclear share of the EU [European Union] energy mix—around 30 percent.

Carbon Dioxide Emissions Are the Major Problem

For this reason, I wholeheartedly support the 'declaration on climate change and nuclear energy'. I'll explain why. In the simplest of terms,

Bob Englehart/The Hartford Courant/CagleCartoons.com.

the phenomenon of climate change is all about management of waste from the energy, transport, household and industrial sectors. Carbon dioxide emissions have to be reduced to next to nothing if we are to halt this planet-threatening process. The life cycle of a nuclear power plant, from conception to decommissioning, emits almost no CO_2 to the atmosphere. All the other primary fuels capable of supplying a significant share of today's energy needs (gas, oil & coal) cannot, as yet, be used without adding to the CO_2 emissions problem.

Opponents of nuclear power claim that nuclear waste is an unsolved problem. It is only a 'problem' at all because all the waste is captured and must be safely contained forever. Only when the equivalent 'problem' is solved for fossil fuels can they continue without spoiling our planet. I hope one day to see a working, commercially viable CO_2 sequestration and storage plant—but today we do not have it.

Renewable Energies Are Inadequate

The same people who oppose nuclear power often promote energy saving, hydro-power, wind power, solar power, hydrogen and the rest. Well I support all those things too—don't we all? But reality tells us that no new large hydro-power dams will be built because they cause other environmental damage. The same can be said for wind-power. Compare the new nuclear plant being built in Finland with a wind equivalent. The best performing wind turbines will achieve their maximum output for 30 per cent of their running time. So the 1600 MW [megawatt] nuclear unit being built in Finland would need at least a 5300 MW wind farm to replace it. The biggest wind turbines today can generate four MW—so who is ready for 1350 windmills next to where they live, where they take their holidays, or even next to where nobody lives? Again, wind can and must make a contribution but it does little to impact on the problem.

Whilst I encourage all renewables, let's get real again, none of them will ever run the Brussels metro system, and if you were going into hospital for an operation you would not like to ask the surgeon, "Is the wind blowing today or is it going to be sunny enough?"

A word on hydrogen: yes, hydrogen cells can produce energy without emissions—the problem is that hydrogen does not exist as a primary fuel. It has to be made and that process is very energy hungry. So unless hydrogen is made by use of nuclear or other non-emitting technologies, it does nothing to reduce the problem. Some other MEPs are promoting a Hydrogen Charter which omits to point this out.

We should also go for more energy efficiency. However, it's ironic that whilst each household and each factory can become more energy efficient, consumption by society as a whole continues to increase. The fact is that as energy efficiency leads to reduced costs, so the homeowner or factory owner buys more (energy or appliances) and the power sector increases production.

Nuclear Energy Is a Safe and Cheap Energy Source

I believe the problems and the solutions for nuclear power are not technical nor environmental but political ones. It's the politicians who will decide the future of the nuclear industry on every continent. This underlines the importance of supporting the MEP declaration on climate change and nuclear energy. Why? Because, quite simply, nuclear power opponents will be active in the political debate and will tell you that nuclear power is dangerous, even though it kills fewer people per kWh [kilowatt hour] than any other technology—almost zero in fact. They argue that it's expensive even though, for new build, it is number two after combined cycle gas which pollutes and creates a dependency on Russia. Opponents say it has no answer to its waste problems even though it is the only bulk supply technology that contains and manages its waste safely, and they will tell you that nuclear is unpopular, yet in a recent opinion poll in Sweden, where they voted 20 years ago to close their nuclear plants, 80 per cent were supportive of nuclear.

Even some Greens are aware of the urgency of the situation. James Lovelock, the Green Guru of the 80's, and best known for his Gaia theory on sustainability, makes a powerful case for nuclear power largely on the grounds that renewable resources could not be introduced quickly enough to avert a greenhouse catastrophe resulting from the use of fossil fuels.

Although wind power is a clean energy source, it is not powerful enough to meet America's energy needs.

Nuclear power is a formidable energy source that can power enormous ships such as this military vessel.

Nuclear Power Is an Environmental Solution

As a one-time marine engineer with a background in power production and, despite being a representative of a coal mining region—when we had pits in Lancashire—I am a supporter of nuclear energy.

The problem is that my support is based on technical and practical arguments—but it is political ones that will win or lose the day. But I support nuclear power primarily from an environmental point of view. . . . You see I want my grandchildren and their grandchildren to live in a world which is clean and fit to live in.

EVALUATING THE AUTHORS' ARGUMENTS:

Wynn supports nuclear power because he claims it does not contribute to global warming. But M. V. Ramana, the author of the following viewpoint, challenges the idea that using nuclear power can reduce global warming. Lay out each author's position and explain which position you agree with.

Viewpoint
6

Nuclear Power Will Not Help Reduce Global Warming

M. V. Ramana

"In reality, several steps in the nuclear fuel cycle . . . emit copious amounts of greenhouse gases."

In the following viewpoint the author argues that nuclear power will not help reduce global warming. He argues that nuclear energy is not entirely free of carbon dioxide emissions since many steps in the nuclear fuel cycle produce emissions. Furthermore, Ramana remains concerned about the problems of nuclear waste and the potential danger nuclear power could pose if it was attacked by terrorists. He concludes that nuclear power should not be mistaken for an environmentally friendly energy source.

M.V. Ramana teaches at the Centre for Interdisciplinary Studies in Environment and Development located in Bangalore, India.

AS YOU READ, CONSIDER THE FOLLOWING QUESTIONS:

1. According to Ramana, what effect did Japan's increase in nuclear energy from 1965 to 1995 have on carbon emissions?

M.V. Ramana, "Nuclear Power: No Solution to Global Warming," wagingpeace.org, July 1, 2005. Reproduced by permission of the *Friday Times*.

2. What does the author believe is the only real solution to preventing global warming?
3. Why does the author feel that nuclear power cannot be used as an interim solution to climate change while better technologies are being sought?

There is simply no way global warming can be stopped without significant reductions in the current energy consumption levels of developed countries. Whatever else one could say about nuclear power in the old days, it was certainly not considered environment-friendly. Over the past few years, however, a number of so-called environmentalists, generally Western, have come out in support of nuclear power as an essential component of any practical solution to global warming. Predictably, flailing nuclear establishments everywhere have grabbed this second opportunity to make a claim for massive state investments and resurrect an industry that has collapsed

Nuclear power plants emit some carbon dioxide, and thus can be considered to be a cause of global warming.

in country after country due to its inability to provide clean, safe, or cheap electricity. But just as the old mantra "too cheap to meter" proved ridiculously wrong, the claims that nuclear energy can contribute significantly to mitigating climate change do not bear scrutiny. . . .

The fact that some environmentalists have endorsed nuclear power as a solution to global warming deserves serious consideration and response. The enormity of the potential impact of climate change adds to this imperative.

Flawed Assumptions
Two implicit but flawed assumptions underlie most claims about the significance of nuclear energy for the climate-change issue. The first is that climate change can be tackled without confronting and

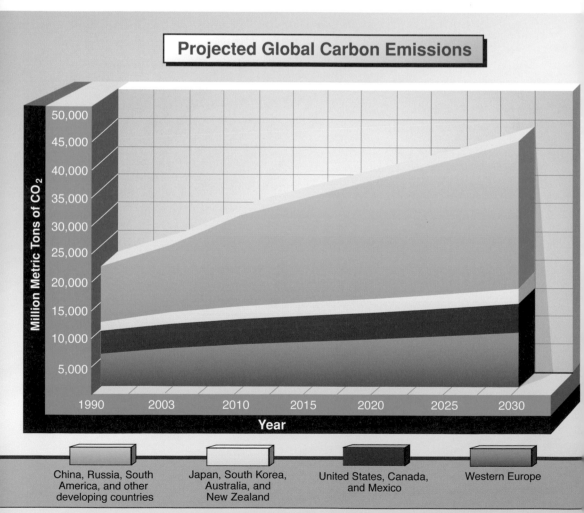

Projected Global Carbon Emissions

Million Metric Tons of CO_2

| China, Russia, South America, and other developing countries | Japan, South Korea, Australia, and New Zealand | United States, Canada, and Mexico | Western Europe |

Note: One metric ton equals 1.1 tons, or 2,204 pounds (1,000 kilograms).

Source: "International Energy Outlook 2006," Energy Information Administration, U.S. Department of Energy, June 2006.

changing Western, especially American, patterns of energy consumption—the primary causes and continuing drivers for unsustainable increases in carbon emissions and global warming. This is plain impossible; there is simply no way global warming can be stopped without significant reductions in the current energy consumption levels of Western/developed countries. Efforts by various developing countries to match these consumption levels only intensify the problem.

FAST FACT

Nuclear waste can remain radioactive for as long as one thousand years.

The second flawed assumption is that the adoption of nuclear power will lower aggregate carbon emissions. In a strictly technical sense, each unit of electricity produced by a nuclear plant would cause the emission of fewer grams of carbon than a unit of electricity generated by thermal plants. (A false myth often propagated by the nuclear lobby is that nuclear energy is carbon free. In reality, several steps in the nuclear fuel cycle, from uranium mining to enrichment to reprocessing, emit copious amounts of greenhouse gases.) And so, the assumption goes, installing a large number of nuclear power stations will lower carbon emission rates.

The problem is that the assumption holds true only if all else remains constant, in particular consumption levels. But that is never the case. In fact, there is no empirical evidence that increased use of nuclear power has contributed to actually reducing a country's carbon dioxide emissions. The best case study is Japan, a strongly pro-nuclear energy country. As Japanese nuclear chemist and winner of the 1997 Right Livelihood Award Jinzaburo Takagi pointed out, from 1965 to 1995 Japan's nuclear plant capacity went from zero to over 40,000 MW [megawatts]. During the same period, carbon dioxide emissions went up from about 400 million tonnes to about 1200 million tonnes.

Nuclear Power Will Not Lower Carbon Emissions

There are two reasons why increased use of nuclear power does not necessarily lower carbon emissions. First, nuclear energy is best suited only to produce baseload electricity. That only constitutes a fraction of all sources of carbon emissions. Other sectors of the

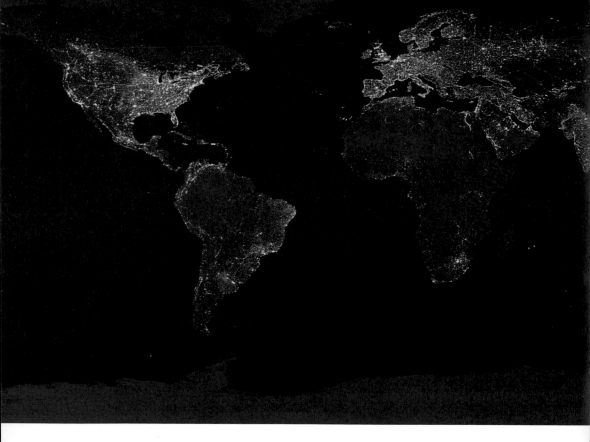

Humans around the world consume enormous amounts of energy—our powerful lights

economy where carbon dioxide and other greenhouse gases are emitted, such as transportation, cannot be operated using electricity from nuclear reactors. This situation is unlikely to change anytime in the near future.

A second and more fundamental reason is provided by John Byrnes of the University of Delaware's Centre for Energy and Environmental Policy, who observed that nuclear technology is an expensive source of energy service and can only be economically viable in a society that relies on increasing levels of energy use. Nuclear power tends to require and promote a supply-oriented energy policy and an energy-intensive pattern of development.

The high cost of nuclear power also means that any potential decreases in carbon emissions due to its adoption are expensive, certainly higher than energy efficiency improvements as well as other means to lower emissions from thermal power plants.

Nuclear Power Is Not the Answer

One other argument advanced by some of these so-called environmentalists is that nuclear power is just an interim solution while better solutions are worked out. The idea is wholly at odds with the history of nuclear establishments around the world and completely underestimates the remarkable capabilities of powerful institutions to find resources for continuing existence and growth. Once such institutions are established, they will find ways to ensure that they are not disempowered.

For nuclear power to make a significant dent in global warming, nuclear capacity must grow manifold (ten-plus). The notion that nuclear power can increase manifold from current levels and then be phased out is wishful thinking, to say the least. Such a projection also completely ignores existing realities—uncompetitive costs, safety concerns, the unresolved problem of radioactive waste, and the link to the bomb—that come in the way of any significant expansion of nuclear power.

Global warming is a serious issue. Providing ill-thought-out answers is no way to address such a grave problem.

EVALUATING THE AUTHORS' ARGUMENTS:

Authors Terry Wynn and M.V. Ramana disagree on whether nuclear power can help reduce global warming. In writing their positions, neither author chose to use quotes in their essays. In your opinion, did this weaken or strengthen their essays? What types of people might each author have quoted to support his position?

Chapter 2

What Problems Might Be Caused by Global Warming?

City traffic is a main source of excess carbon dioxide in the atmosphere, which could lead to global warming.

Global Warming Causes More Intense Hurricane Activity

Derrick Z. Jackson

"Research continues to increasingly tie global warming to an increase in the intensity of tropical storms."

Global warming is causing more intense hurricanes, according to the author of the following viewpoint. He notes that the percentage of big storms and the duration of storms are increasing. He warns that storms more severe than Hurricanes Katrina and Rita, which ravaged the United States Gulf Coast in 2005, can be expected over the next century as the climate continues to warm.

Derrick Z. Jackson is an award-winning columnist for the *Boston Globe*. In 2001 he was a finalist for the Pulitzer Prize in commentary.

AS YOU READ, CONSIDER THE FOLLOWING QUESTIONS:

1. According to the author, what percentage of contemporary storms are classified as category 4 and 5 storms?

2. How much have ocean temperatures risen since the 1970s, as reported by Jackson?
3. What does the National Oceanic and Atmospheric Administration Web site suggest might cause more intense hurricanes over the next century?

As the media screams about the one-two punch of Hurricanes Katrina and Rita, the question becomes how many more times does America need to be knocked to the canvas before we answer the bell on global warming.

The only talk from our leaders is about rebuilding. In his address to the nation from a ghostly New Orleans, President Bush said, "When one resident of this city who lost his home was asked by a reporter if he would relocate he said, 'Naw, I will rebuild but I'll build higher.' That is our vision of the future, in this city and beyond. We will not just rebuild, we will build higher and better."

It figures that Bush would talk about building higher in the lowest city in the United States, in a presidency where he has ignored the rising waters of the planet. He said, "Americans have never left our destiny to the whims of nature and we will not start now."

The Connection Between Hurricanes and Global Warming

Actually, there is no better time to start understanding that nature is at the mercy of our whimsy. Our destiny depends on it.

In this tragic season of hurricanes, research continues to increasingly tie global warming to an increase in the intensity of tropical storms.

One was published last month in the journal *Nature* by Kerry Emanuel, a professor of atmospheric science at the Massachusetts Institute of Technology. Another was published last week in the journal *Science* by atmospheric researchers at Georgia Tech and the National Center for Atmospheric Research.

Percentage of Intense Storms on the Rise

While there has been no increase in the actual number of storms worldwide, the Georgia Tech/NCAR study found the number of hurricanes that reached categories 4 and 5, with winds of at least

131 miles per hour, have gone from comprising 20 percent of hurricanes in the 1970s to 35 percent today. This is with only a half-degree centigrade rise in tropical surface water temperatures.

The percentage of big storms in the North Atlantic has increased from 20 percent to 25 percent. The rise is much worse in the rest of

President George W. Bush surveys damage in New Orleans after Hurricane Katrina. Global warming is believed to cause an increase in powerful storms.

the world, where millions of less fortunate people cannot flee the coast in SUVs on interstate roads.

In the 1970s, no ocean basin saw more than 25 percent of hurricanes become a 4 or 5. Today, that percentage is 34, 35, and 41 percent, respectively, in the South Indian, East Pacific, and West Pacific oceans. The biggest jump was in the Southwestern Pacific, from 8 percent to 25 percent.

Emanuel, who formerly doubted that hurricane intensity was tied to global warming, said that he was stunned when his research showed that just that half-degree rise in tropical ocean temperatures has also seen a 50 percent rise in average storm peak winds in the North Atlantic and East and West Pacific in the last half century.

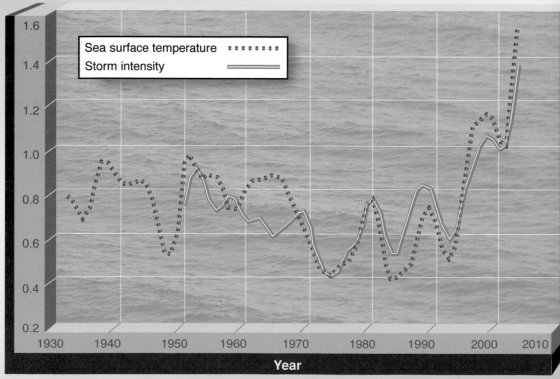

Hurricane Intensity and Ocean Temperature

A study published in the journal *Nature* shows that as ocean surface temperatures increase, hurricanes become more intense.

Source: Kerry Emanuel, "Increasing Destructiveness of Tropical Cyclones over the Past 30 Years," *Nature*, August 4, 2005.

Duration of Storms Increasing

The accumulated annual duration of storms in the North Atlantic and the western North Pacific has shot up by 60 percent.

"I wasn't looking for global warming," Emanuel said by cell phone in Spain where he is conducting research on Mediterranean storms. "But it stuck out like a sore thumb."

Emanuel originally thought that a half-degree rise in ocean temperatures should have resulted in wind speeds much lower than that. Emanuel said he hoped the more recent findings would be taken as a signal for action. The average hurricane, he said, releases the equivalent of worldwide electrical capacity. Hurricanes Katrina and Rita are 10 times stronger.

Not surprisingly, these new findings have drawn skepticism from scientists who cling to past climate models and flat denials from a Bush administration that has all but censored serious talk about global warming.

> # FAST FACT
>
> The deadliest natural disaster in the United States was the 1900 hurricane in Galveston, Texas, with an estimated eight thousand dead.

Stronger Storms Expected

The National Oceanic and Atmospheric Administration's website says, "The strongest hurricanes in the present climate may be upstaged by even more intense hurricanes over the next century as the earth's climate is warmed by increasing levels of greenhouse gases,"

But Max Mayfield, director of NOAA's National Hurricane Center, testified [in 2005] before a Senate committee that increased hurricane activity "is due to natural fluctuations" and is "not enhanced substantially by global warming."

The one-two punch of Katrina and Rita does not yet have us reaching for the smelling salts. We are still waiting for global warming to hit us below the belt.

EVALUATING THE AUTHORS' ARGUMENTS:

In this viewpoint, the author warns that our destiny depends on a better understanding of nature. Considering what you know about global warming, do you think this an accurate or an overly dramatic statement? Explain your reasoning.

Viewpoint 2

Global Warming Does Not Cause More Intense Hurricane Activity

"There is little or no rigorous scientific evidence global warming has contributed anything significant to the recent strong hurricane seasons."

Charles C.W. Cooke and Alex Kormendi

The theory linking more intense hurricanes with global warming is flawed, according to the authors of the following viewpoint. Charles C.W. Cooke and Alex Kormendi point out that hurricane activity has increased and decreased over time, and in periods prior to human activities that are thought to cause global warming. Furthermore, hurricane activity has not increased equally around the world, and the authors take this as proof that global warming is not responsible for increased hurricane activity.

Cooke and Kormendi are research associates at the Competitive Enterprise Institute, a nonprofit public policy organization.

With America's eyes fixed on Hurricane Katrina's destructive force, we naturally look for an explanation or a cause. Eyes in times past would have roved upward to the heavens; now they fix themselves firmly on science, eager to hear explanations of a link between global warming and impressive natural disasters.

There are many out there ready to indulge this notion and use a terrible calamity to further their own political ends. They glibly contend hurricanes are exactly the sort of result we can expect if we keep contributing to global warming and that New Orleans has reaped the fruit of our irresponsibility.

Chief among this new band of augurs is Robert F. Kennedy Jr., who has directly blamed President Bush and Mississippi Gov. Haley Barbour for the destruction caused by Katrina. He is working in tandem with self-proclaimed expert Ross Gelbspan who suggests the link between global warming and the disaster is so clear the hurricane should be re-named "Global Warming."

Both cite Kerry Emanuel of the Massachusetts Institute of Technology, who recently published a paper arguing there is a clear correlation between climate change and hurricanes. As man warms the oceans, the argument says, hurricanes intensify and cause greater damage. The result: More houses and property destroyed and damaged and higher insurance costs.

Hurricane Cycles Are Natural

Yet there is much evidence this is all just hot air. The alarmists notably fail to cite the cyclical nature of hurricane behavior. From the late 1920s to the 1960s there was high hurricane activity. If global warming is to blame for more hurricanes now, what caused the last cycle?

Satellite imagery shows Hurricane Katrina approaching the Gulf Coast. Some scientists believe that powerful storms are part of the earth's natural weather cycles.

As leading hurricane scientist William Gray argues, North Atlantic surface temperatures vary naturally. They were cool from the 1970s to the 1990s, but warm during the last period of intense hurricane activity from the late '20s to the 1960s. He says, "Instead of seeing a long-term trend up or down, we do see a quasicyclic multi-decade regime that alternates between active and quiet phases for major Atlantic hurricanes on the scale of 25–40 years each."

Flawed Reasoning

The global warming–hurricane theory is flawed; Mr. Emanuel and others have tracked the buildup of a natural cycle, not discovered a

Hurricanes Through History

The number and intensity of hurricanes all over the world have noticeably increased during the past decade (category 4 and 5 hurricanes are the strongest on the intensity scale). Some scientists believe these increases may be part of a natural trend that occurs over longer periods of time, and that further studies are needed before we know whether or not they are related to global warming.

Ocean Basin	Period			
	1975–1989		1990–2004	
	Number of Hurricanes	Percentage of Category 4 and 5 Hurricanes	Number of Hurricanes	Percentage of Category 4 and 5 Hurricanes
East Pacific	36	25	49	35
West Pacific	85	25	116	41
North Atlantic	16	20	25	25
Southwestern Pacific	10	12	22	28
North Indian	1	8	7	25
South Indian	23	18	50	34

Source: "Changes in Tropical Cyclone Number, Duration, and Intensity in a Warming Environment," *Science*, September 16, 2005.

linear trend. It is apparent the intuitive ideas forwarded by the likes of Mr. Emanuel inevitably result from classic "cherry picking" science. Given that patterns in hurricanes seem driven by 20–40 year cycles, to draw solid conclusions from a period that began in the 1970s and neglect prior natural patterns is a bit like staying up from 5 A.M. to 9 A.M. and finding there is a trend the Earth is getting brighter.

Further, global warming alarmists contradict their own scientific case. If, as the models suggest, warming occurs mostly toward the poles, the north-south temperature gradient should narrow. If this is so, the frequency and intensity of hurricanes should diminish. If they believe their own science, the alarmists should argue global warming is reducing hurricanes.

And there is no answer forthcoming why, if global warming is to blame, its results seem to specifically target the Atlantic and ignore the Pacific and Indian oceans.

Rising Property Damage Costs Are Misleading

It is equally misleading to use rising property damage costs to suggest increased hurricane intensity. It is true there is more property destroyed in hurricanes now than 50 years ago. This is not, however, due to hurricanes getting stronger but of more property development being in their paths.

According to Christopher Landsea of the National Oceanic and Atmospheric Administration, "Southeast Florida including metropolitan Miami went 42 years (1950–1992) between strikes by intense hurricanes. During that time, the population increased by more than 600 percent."

Even if hurricane intensity declined, economic damage would rise. In a 1996 paper titled "Downward trends in the frequency of intense Atlantic hurricanes during the past five decades," Mr. Landsea argued a "large

Larry Wright. © 2005 Larry Wright. Reproduced by permission of Cagle Cartoons, Inc.

portion of [the] immense toll" of high-profile hurricanes "is due to the property development and population increases along the U.S coastal states."

There is little or no rigorous scientific evidence global warming has contributed anything significant to the recent strong hurricane seasons, yet alarmists—including some scientists who should know better—continue making the link.

Even Kerry Emanuel told the British newspaper the *Independent* he didn't think Katrina could be blamed on global warming. In days past, Katrina would have been called an Act of God. Today some, for the basest political reasons, want to call it an act of man. Our forefathers were nearer the truth.

EVALUATING THE AUTHORS' ARGUMENTS:

The authors of this viewpoint disagree with the author of the previous viewpoint over whether global warming is responsible for an increase in hurricane activity. After reading both viewpoints, what is your opinion on the connection between global warming and hurricane activity? Explain your answer using evidence from the text.

Global Warming Will Raise Sea Levels

Richard A. Kerr

"The apparent sensitivity of ice sheets to a warmer world could prove disastrous."

In the following viewpoint Richard A. Kerr argues that global warming will cause glaciers to melt, resulting in a rise in sea levels around the globe. This will cause coastal areas to drown, resulting in loss of habitat and extensive property damage. Though scientists are unsure exactly how much sea levels will rise, Kerr warns that efforts should be immediately taken to prevent global warming and the melting of glaciers.

Richard A. Kerr has written about earth and planetary sciences since 1977 for *Science*, a magazine published by the American Association for the Advancement of Science.

AS YOU READ, CONSIDER THE FOLLOWING QUESTIONS:

1. What three places might be affected by rising sea levels, according to Kerr?
2. What is causing some glaciers to move faster, as reported by the author?

Richard A. Kerr, "A Worrying Trend of Less Ice, Higher Seas," *Science*, vol. 311, March 24, 2006, pp. 1698–1700. Copyright 2006 by AAAS. Reproduced by permission.

Have an urge lately to run for higher ground? That would be understandable, given all the talk about the world's ice melting into the sea. Kilimanjaro's ice cloak is soon to disappear, the summertime Arctic Ocean could be ice-free by century's end, 11,000-year-old ice shelves around Antarctica are breaking up over the course of weeks, and glaciers there and in Greenland have begun galloping into the sea. All true. And the speeding glaciers, at least, are surely driving up sea level and pushing shorelines inland.

Speeding Glaciers

Scientists may not be heading for the hills just yet, but they're increasingly worried. Not about their beach houses being inundated anytime soon; they're worried about what they've missed. Some of the glaciers draining the great ice sheets of Antarctica and Greenland have sped up dramatically, driving up sea level and catching scientists unawares. They don't fully understand what is happening. And if they don't understand what a little warming is doing to the ice sheets today, they reason, what can they say about ice's fate and rising seas in the greenhouse world of the next century or two?

That uncertainty is unsettling. Climatologists know that, as the world warmed in the past, "by some process, ice sheets got smaller," says glaciologist Robert Bindschadler of NASA's Goddard Space Flight Center in Greenbelt, Maryland. But "we didn't know the process; I think we're seeing it now. And it's not gradual." Adds geoscientist Michael Oppenheimer of Princeton University, "The time scale for future loss of most of an ice sheet may not be millennia," as glacier models have suggested, "but centuries."

Melting Glaciers Equals Rising Sea Level

The apparent sensitivity of ice sheets to a warmer world could prove disastrous. The greenhouse gases that people are spewing into the atmosphere this century might guarantee enough warming to destroy the West Antarctic and Greenland ice sheets, says Oppenheimer, possibly as quickly as within several centuries. That would drive up sea level 5 to 10 meters at rates not seen since the end of the last ice age. New Orleans would flood, for good, as would most of South Florida and much of the Netherlands. Rising seas would push half a billion people inland. "This is not an experiment you get to run twice," says Oppenheimer. "I find this very disturbing."

Much of the world's ice may be shrinking under the growing warmth of the past several decades, but some ice losses will have more dramatic effects on sea level than others. Glaciologists worried about rising sea level are keying on the glaciers

Dwindling Glaciers

Muir Glacier, Glacier Bay, Alaska

1941

2004

Grinnell Glacier, Glacier National Park, Montana

1900

1998

draining the world's two dominant ice reservoirs, Greenland and Antarctica. Summertime Arctic Ocean ice may be on its way out, but its melting does nothing to increase the volume of ocean water; that ice is already floating in the ocean. The same goes for floating ice shelves around Antarctica. The meltwater from receding mountain glaciers and ice caps is certainly raising sea level, but not much. . . .

Greenland Is Losing Ice

As glaciers draining the Greenland Ice Sheet are picking up speed, researchers are realizing that nothing has made up for the increased loss of ice. Greenland's pile of ice is getting smaller. How much smaller is still being debated, if only because of the vast scope of an ice sheet. What goes out through glaciers is just one part of the equation: Ice sheets also lose mass by melting and gain it from snowfall. To gauge those gains and losses Rignot and Kanagaratnam [scientists who used radar to measure the speed of glaciers] used previously published estimates of how the warming climate over Greenland has increased meltwater losses and slightly increased snowfall, making

"HOW ON EARTH DO WE TURN IT OFF?"

The Shrinking Polar Ice Cap

A recent NASA study shows that the North Polar ice cap has been decreasing at a rate of nine percent per decade since the 1970s.

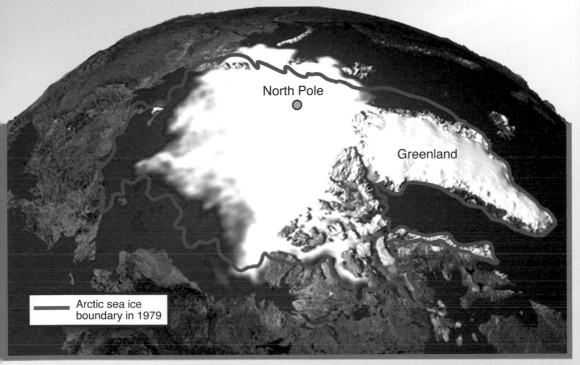

Source: Scientific Visualizations Studio, NASA Goddard Space Flight Center, 2003.

for a growing net loss in addition to the glacier flow. All told, the scientists find that the loss of mass from Greenland doubled from 1996 to 2005. . . .

All things considered, it seems clear that "Greenland has been shifting to a negative mass balance the last few years," says glaciologist Richard Alley of Pennsylvania State University in State College. The same can be said for the West Antarctic Ice Sheet. All recent surveys have the far more massive East Antarctic Ice Sheet slowly gaining mass from increased snowfall. But that gain falls far short of compensating for the loss from West Antarctica. . . .

How Much Will Sea Level Rise?

If the recent behavior of ice sheets is not fully understood, their future is largely a blank. "We don't actually understand what's driving these higher velocities," says [Julian Dowdeswell, a glaciologist from the University of Cambridge], so "it's difficult to say whether that's going to continue," or spread.

At the moment, ice loss from Greenland and West Antarctica combined is contributing less than half of the ongoing 2-millimeters-per-year rise in sea level; the rest comes from melting mountain glaciers and the simple thermal expansion of seawater. If the recent surge of ice to the sea continues, sea level might reach something like half a meter higher by 2100. That would be substantial but not catastrophic. To produce really scary rises really fast (say, a meter or more per century), the air and water will have to continue warming in the right—or wrong—places. The temperature rise will have to spread northward around Greenland and in the south around West Antarctica, reaching the big ice shelves where most of that ice sheet drains. And glacier accelerations triggered near the sea must propagate far inland to draw on the bulk of an ice sheet. . . .

No one knows whether the exceptionally strong warmings around the ice will continue apace, whether the ice accelerations of recent years will slow as the ice sheets adjust to the new warmth, or whether more glaciers will fall prey to the warmth. No one knows yet.

EVALUATING THE AUTHORS' ARGUMENTS:

The author of this viewpoint cites the work of several scientists to support his belief that global warming is melting glaciers and thereby raising sea levels. In what way does quoting these sources lend credibility to his argument?

Global Warming Will Lower Sea Levels

World Climate Report

"*The snow and ice cover over large portions of Antarctica has been increasing, leading to a drawdown of global sea level.*"

The *World Climate Report* is a biweekly on-line publication of New Hope Environmental Services, Inc., a science consulting firm. In the following viewpoint the authors argue that global warming, if real, would actually lower sea levels rather than raise them, at least in Antarctica. They reason that when sea temperatures rise, more water evaporates from the oceans. It then falls as snow over Antarctica, adding to the ice cap's size. This draws moisture from the sea, lowering water levels. The authors further point out that any decrease in southern sea levels is kept in check by nature's ability to regulate itself. They conclude that predictions of rising or lowering sea levels are nothing but global warming hysteria.

AS YOU READ, CONSIDER THE FOLLOWING QUESTIONS:

1. According to Curt Davis, how many tons of snow per year did Antarctica gain between 1991 and 2003?

"Antarctic Ice: A Global Warming Snow Job?" *World Climate Report*, May 27, 2005. Reproduced by permission.

2. Why do the authors reject warming theories based upon observations of the Antarctic Peninsula?

3. According to the authors, how does the rate of sea-level rise in Greenland compare to the sea-level drop in Antarctica? How do the authors interpret these numbers?

C limate scientists have long suspected that warming the oceans around a very cold continent is likely to dramatically increase snowfall. Consider Antarctica. It's plenty chilly, dozens of degrees below freezing, and it's surrounded by water. The warmer the water, the greater the evaporation from its surface, and, obviously, the more moisture it contributes to the local atmosphere.

So, when this moisture gets swirled up by a common cyclone, do you think it's going to fall as *rain* in Antarctica?

A recent study, no shocker to real climatologists (but perhaps to climate doomsayers), demonstrates this simple physics. It appears in the latest *ScienceExpress*, and it shows that the vast majority of the Antarctic landmass is rapidly gaining ice and snow cover.

Obviously this moisture comes from the sea. And, being deposited in solid form on the land-way-down-under, this lowers the earth's sea level. . . .

Positive Changes

Recent climate changes have led to a fairly large warming trend in the region around the Antarctic Peninsula—the spit of land that stretches from the Antarctic mainland towards the southern tip of South America. In this region, comprising about 2 percent of the entirety of Antarctica, significant changes associated with rising temperatures are being observed—floating ice shelves are breaking up, glaciers are shrinking, seal species are moving in, grasses, tiny shrubs and mosses are thriving, etc. By most accounts, transitioning from a relatively barren, frozen landscape to a warmer, less frozen one would seem to be

FAST FACT

From 1992 to 2003 East Antarctica gained ice mass at the average rate of 45 billion tons per year.

a positive development, as this change presents a growing opportunity for increased species richness and diversity. But, in today's world, dominated by an eagerness to demonstrate how human activities are impacting the innocent "natural" species of the world, all change is bad.

The fact is that the vast majority of global warming stories that have come out of Antarctica are based upon observations and events on and around the Peninsula. . . . Indeed, the number of stories about Antarctic melting is roughly in inverse proportion to the percentage of the Antarctic continent that they pertain to (and thus their global significance). For instance, most of Antarctica has actually been cooling for the past couple of decades. And now comes word that the snow and ice cover over large portions of Antarctica has been increasing, leading to a drawdown of global sea level.

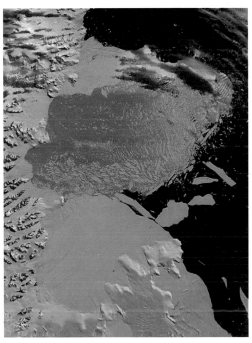

Satellite imagery shows the Larsen B ice shelf collapsing, due possibly to global warming.

Increased Snowfall

In their *ScienceExpress* article, Curt Davis (University of Missouri-Columbia) and his collaborators used satellite radar altimetry measurements from 1992 to 2003 to determine that, on average, the elevation of about 8.5 million square kilometers of the Antarctic interior has been increasing. The increasing elevation was then linked to increases in snowfall, which was translated into a mass gain of 38–52 billion tons per year, tying up enough moisture to lower sea level by [0.10–0.14] millimeters per year.

(The study region covered about 70 percent of the total ice sheet area—the satellites couldn't "see" all the way to the South Pole due to orbital constraints, and the altimetry doesn't work well in areas of rough terrain such as along the coastline).

This 0.12 millimeters is a very fortuitous number. In 2000, NASA iceman William Krabill grabbed global headlines by claiming that melting in the world's other big icebox—Greenland—was raising sea level by 0.13 millimeters annually. . . .

It seems perfectly logical that a warming of the Southern Oceans (as opposed to most of the Antarctic continent proper where tem-

Gains and Losses in Antarctic Ice

Though parts of the miles-thick ice sheet in East Antarctica are actively thickening (+ symbols), West Antarctica's ice is thinning (− symbols). Larger symbols indicate a greater volume of thickening or thinning.

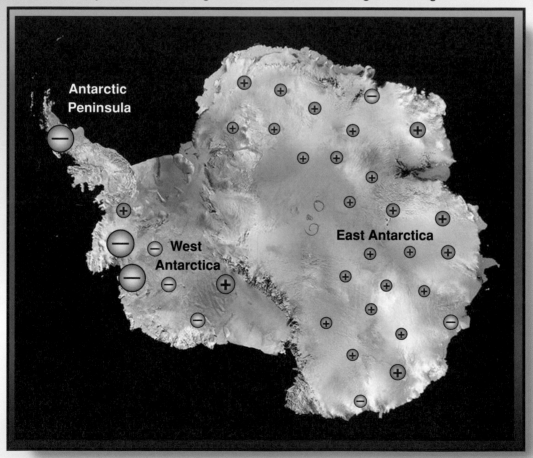

Satellites measuring Antarctica since 1992 have helped scientists estimate that overall, about 152 cubic kilometers of Antarctic ice (over 40 trillion gallons of water) are lost each year.

Sources: D.G. Vaughn, "How Does the Antarctic Ice Sheet Affect Sea Level Rise?" *Science*, 308, 2005; NASA/German Aerospace Center Gravity Recovery and Climate Experiment (GRACE), March 2006.

peratures have been decreasing) has led to higher levels of atmospheric moisture that eventually precipitates out over Antarctica. The authors caution though, that from their work alone, it is impossible to tell whether the observed snowfall increases are from natural climate variations or from a human-induced global warming.

Just for the hey of it, assume the increased snow cover *is* because of anthropogenic global warming. That would be more evidence that the global climate system has more checks and balances in it than the U.S. Constitution, something as obvious as this planet's propensity to sustain life for three billion years.

EVALUATING THE AUTHORS' ARGUMENTS:

The authors of this viewpoint have faith in the planet's ability to regulate itself and keep its systems in natural balance. The authors of other viewpoints in this book believe that human activities have eroded the planet's ability to regulate itself. What is your opinion on this debate? Support your answer with evidence from the text.

Global Warming Will Increase the World's Food Supply

H. Sterling Burnett

"The best available evidence indicates a warmer planet should result in bountiful crops."

Global warming will increase the world's food supply, according to H. Sterling Burnett, author of the following viewpoint. Burnett believes that global warming will result in longer growing seasons, more abundant rainfall, and decreases in crop-killing frosts—conditions that will allow crops to thrive. Burnett also explains that more carbon dioxide, another feature of global warming, will speed the growth of plants. Burnett concludes that global warming could therefore benefit the world's hungry populations.

Burnett is a senior fellow for the National Center for Policy Analysis, a non-profit public policy research institute.

AS YOU READ, CONSIDER THE FOLLOWING QUESTIONS:

1. According to Burnett, how did the current warming trend affect vegetation?

H. Sterling Burnett, "Warming: Famine or Feast?" E-Team Web Log, May 25, 2005. Reproduced by permission.

2. How much has atmospheric carbon dioxide increased in the last half century, according to Burnett?

3. According to the author, carbon dioxide enrichment causes plants to develop more extensive root systems. How does this benefit plants?

Mass famine and starvation due to a collapse of agricultural production ranks high among myriad catastrophes environmentalists claim human-induced global warming will cause. Fortunately, this is one global warming bogeyman that's easy to slay.

Regardless of the cause of the current warming, the best available evidence indicates a warmer planet should result in bountiful crops. The modest warming many scientists expect should result in longer growing seasons, more sunshine and rainfall, while summertime high temperatures change little. And a warmer planet means milder winters and fewer crop-killing frosts. History shows the Earth's climate is less stormy and more stable in relatively warm eras.

The Benefits of Increased Rainfall

The present warming trend has not resulted in agricultural water shortages. Indeed, rainfall is increasing moderately over most of the world because global warming evaporates more water from the oceans, where it falls back down to earth in a reinvigorated hydrological cycle.

Thanks partly to increased rainfall, infrared satellite readings show worldwide vegetative activity generally increased 6.17 percent between 1982 and 1999. The world is getting greener. Continued warming should increase, rather than reduce, rainfall.

The Benefits of Increased Carbon Dioxide

In addition, global warming also increases carbon dioxide (CO_2), which acts like fertilizer for plants. As the planet warms, oceans naturally release huge tonnages of additional CO_2. (Cold water can hold much more of a gas than warmer water).

CO_2 in the atmosphere has increased more than 30 percent in the past half-century. CO_2 is a critical component of photosynthesis, the process by which plants use sunlight to create carbohydrates—the material that makes up their root and body structures. Increasing CO_2 levels not only speeds the growth of plants, it improves their water use efficiency. More CO_2 also decreases water loss in plants, which is beneficial in arid climates or during droughts.

Plants Grow Well in Greenhouses

Botanists pump large volumes of CO_2 into their greenhouses to enhance plant growth. A series of 55 experiments by research scientist Sherwood Idso, formerly of the Agriculture Department, support

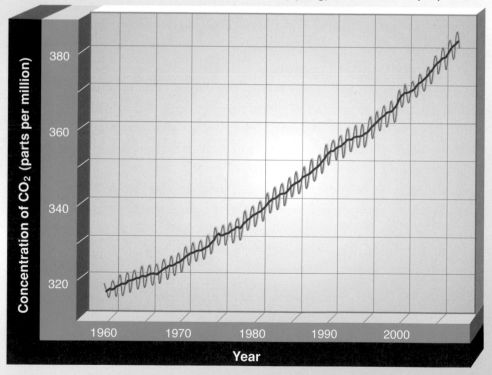

Carbon Dioxide in the Atmosphere

Carbon dioxide (CO_2) measurements have been taken every month since 1958 in the atmosphere over Mauna Loa Observatory, Hawaii. The smooth red curve represents the average between each year's maximum (spring) and minimum (fall) levels.

Source: Scripps Institute of Oceanography/National Oceanic and Atmospheric Administration, September 2006.

A technician compares plants grown with varying carbon dioxide levels. By some accounts, excess carbon dioxide stimulates plants and helps them grow.

botanists' faith in CO_2's beneficial effects. For example, when Mr. Idso increased CO_2 by 300 parts per million (ppm) above the current atmospheric level of more than 370 ppm, plant growth increased 31 percent under optimal water conditions, and 63 percent under water scarcity. With a 600 ppm CO_2 increase, plant growth

What Problems Might Be Caused by Global Warming? 85

was enhanced 51 percent under optimal water conditions and an astonishing 219 percent under conditions of water shortage.

CO_2 enrichment causes plants to develop more extensive root systems that allow plants to reach additional pockets of both water and nutrients in the soil, reducing the metabolic energy required to capture vital nutrients. More extensive, active roots also stimulate and enhance the activity of bacteria and other organisms in the soil that are beneficial to plants.

More CO_2, More Crops

Since many of today's plants evolved when CO_2 levels were much higher, some scientists fear today's plants are literally starving from CO_2 deprivation.

Based on nearly 800 scientific observations around the world, a doubling of CO_2 from present levels would improve plant productivity on average by 32 percent across species. Controlled experiments have shown that, that under elevated CO_2 levels, average yields of cereal grains, including rice, wheat and oats are 25 percent to 64 percent higher. Tubers and root crops, including potatoes and cassava, yield 18 to 75 percent more under high CO_2 conditions. And yields of legumes, including peas, beans and soybeans, increase between 28 percent and 46 percent.

> **FAST FACT**
>
> At temperatures higher than 96.8 degrees Fahrenheit, peanut yields drop about 10 percent per degree of temperature increase, according to researcher Hartwell Allen.

So far, since 1950, in a period of global warming, these factors have helped the world's grain production soar from 700 million to more than 2 billion tons [in 2004].

Humans can help nature along. Recently, Egypt genetically engineered a drought-tolerant wheat plant—containing a gene from the barley plant—that needs to be irrigated only once, rather than eight times per season. The new wheat is expected to dramatically increase food production in semi-arid climates. In addition, constantly improving transportation systems help reduce localized food shortages.

We Should Fear Ice, Not Warmth

The real famine threat will come not in the present warming, but rather the next Ice Age when huge ice sheets will once again cover Canada and Russia, and the Northern Plains will be too cold to farm. Fortunately, that test may not come for another 10,000 years. By then, unless regulations interfere, the world should have genetically engineered a set of even higher-yielding and still more stress-tolerant crop varieties to feed humanity on dramatically reduced acreage.

EVALUATING THE AUTHORS' ARGUMENTS:

In this viewpoint the author cites research experiments that were conducted on rice, wheat, and other crops to argue that global warming helps plants grow. In the following viewpoint the author cites research experiments on the same kinds of crops to argue that global warming hurts plant growth. After reading both viewpoints, how might you explain this discrepancy?

Global Warming Will Decrease the World's Food Supply

"Since the turn of the millennium, the amount of grain held in the world's stockpiles has been falling."

Martin Mittelstaedt

According to Martin Mittelstaedt, the author of the following viewpoint, global warming drastically damages crop production. Over the last several years stockpiles of grain have been significantly lowered worldwide; Mittelstaedt attributes this to steadily warmer temperatures caused by global warming. The author argues that warmer temperatures reduce a plant's ability to fertilize its seeds. He warns that global warming will cause further reductions in harvests and supplies, which will lead to a worldwide hunger crisis.

Mittelstaedt is an environmental reporter for the Toronto *Globe and Mail*, a daily newspaper in Canada.

AS YOU READ, CONSIDER THE FOLLOWING QUESTIONS:

1. According to the author, how much grain was in the world's stockpiles at the end of the 2003 harvest? How much did the 1999 harvest yield?

2. What does the word "larder" mean in the context of this view-point?
3. What did scientists at the International Rice Research Institute discover about rice seeds, as described in the viewpoint?

E ach year around [spring] time, farmers across the breadbaskets of the Northern Hemisphere hop on their tractors and drive out to their fields, full of hope for the new season's grain crop. For the past four years, their efforts haven't been too successful.

It has been an almost unprecedented run of misfortune: four back-to-back meagre harvests, as heat waves, drought and pestilence took their toll—something that hasn't happened since at least 1960.

Dwindling Grain Stockpiles

As a result, since the turn of the millennium, the amount of grain held in the world's stockpiles has been falling. At the end of the 2003 harvest, the amount of wheat, corn, rice and other grains had fallen to about 280 million tonnes. In 1999, it was more than 500 million.

That seems like a lot of grain because bakers can make about 2,000 loaves for every tonne of wheat milled into flour. But considering that the grain has to support both the world's human population and its billions of livestock, there is precious little to go around.

Measured against consumption, there is enough grain left in the planetary larder to last for only 59 days, one of the lower figures on record. After it is used up, people will go hungry if the next harvest fails.

The string of bad harvests hasn't attracted widespread attention yet, but it has the almost undivided attention of Lester Brown, one of the more thoughtful—and controversial—environmentalists in the United States. The founder of the influential Worldwatch Institute, a think tank based in Washington, D.C., believes that the line of bad harvests is no fluke of nature, but rather a harbinger of what one writer has termed "gastronomical Armageddon"—a chaotic and pro-tracted period of food shortages triggered by the world's environmental plagues, including global warming and water shortages.

Increased temperatures could damage wheat and other grain crops, causing a global food shortage.

Food Crisis Inevitable

Environmentalists have long fretted about such things as clear-cutting, species extinction, rain-forest destruction and melting ice caps. But, as important as these issues may be, Mr. Brown thinks that the biggest flashpoint for environment problems is on the world's farms.

The shrinkage of the food supply will be where environmental degradation will have a huge impact on people, he says. "Rising food prices may be the first global economic indicator to signal serious trouble in the relationship between us and the Earth's natural systems and resources," he says.

Mr. Brown thinks that some sort of food crisis is almost inevitable because the magnitude of the exhaustion of grain stockpiles has been staggering. It's equal to about five years of the entire grain output of Canada, one of the top agricultural exporters.

The harvest shortfalls have become so immense, he says, it would take superlative crops in prime agricultural regions this year and next to even begin to start refilling the larder. "I think the chances of farmers digging their way out of this hole are less than one in 10."

Mr. Brown believes that three main environmental trends are threatening to show up, like an unwelcome guest, at humanity's dinner table: global warming, water shortages in many parts of the world and farmland degradation in China. . . .

Effect of High Temperatures

Global warming could be such a threat to food supplies because of the pernicious impact that searing summer temperatures have on the ability of plants to fertilize their seeds, cutting crop yields. Although it is scary to contemplate, new research shows that it wouldn't take much warming from current summer high temperatures to cause almost complete crop failures.

The research, based on tests in the tropics where hot weather is common shows that as temperatures rise above 30 degrees [Celsius]

Rising temperatures could significantly reduce rice yields—the staple crop in Asia and other parts of the world.

when plants flower, the yields of rice, wheat and corn—the staples of the human diet—begin to fall. Although it doesn't work exactly the same way for all crops, there is a drop of about 10 per cent in yield for every one-degree increase.

Readings above 30 degrees [Celsius] amount to a hot summer day in most areas of southern Canada, and are experienced only occasionally. But the same could have been said of Europe—until [2003]. Much of Europe's grain belt had a sneak preview of what warming can do as temperatures soared above the thermal optimum for plant growth over wide areas.

"Those off-the-chart temperatures in Europe, the ones that took 35,000 lives in nine countries, those temperatures shrunk harvests in every country from France east to Ukraine," Mr. Brown says.

His thinking has also been influenced by a refinement of the temperature research that has been conducted at the International Rice Research Institute in the Philippines. Scientists there have found that the fertilization of rice seeds falls from 100 per cent at 34 degrees [Celsius] to near zero at 40 degrees [Celsius].

Rising temperatures may be one reason that world grain harvests have either fallen, or stagnated for the past eight years.

EVALUATING THE AUTHORS' ARGUMENTS:

In his viewpoint the author discusses crop shortages and blames them on global warming and water shortages. How do you think the author of the previous viewpoint, H. Sterling Burnett, would respond to this? Which author do you think is right about the effect of global warming on food supplies?

Facts About Global Warming

Facts About Global Temperatures

- Over the last century global temperatures have risen on average approximately one degree Fahrenheit.
- The warmest decade on record was the 1990s. (Record keeping began in the mid-1800s.)
- Global temperatures are projected to rise an additional three to ten degrees Fahrenheit, according to the United Nations Intergovernmental Panel on Climate Change (IPCC).
- In Alaska, western Canada, and eastern Russia, average temperatures have increased by four to seven degrees Fahrenheit over the last fifty years, according to a recent Arctic Climate Impact Assessment report. This is a much higher rate than the average global temperature rise.
- The rise in global temperatures has not been uniform. Some areas, including parts of the southeastern United States, have cooled over the last century.

Facts About the Kyoto Treaty

- The Kyoto Protocol is a treaty created in 1997 that requires industrialized nations to reduce their levels of greenhouse gases according to specific amounts and specific schedules.
- The Kyoto Protocol took effect on February 16, 2005.
- The United States and Australia are the only two of the thirty-six participating countries who have not yet ratified the treaty.

Facts About Greenhouse Gases

- The major greenhouse gases are water vapor, carbon dioxide, and methane.
- The largest emitter of greenhouse gases is the United States. In 2004 U.S. emissions had increased 15.8 percent since 1990.

- According to the National Climatic Data Center, the level of carbon dioxide in the atmosphere today is the highest in at least 420,000 years.
- Most of the carbon dioxide produced by human activities comes from burning coal, oil, and gas for energy.

Facts About Polar Ice Caps and Sea Levels

- Average global sea level has risen by four to eight inches over the last century, according to the IPCC.
- The IPCC's 2001 report predicts that sea level could rise between four and thirty-five inches over the next century.
- The Greenland ice sheet contains enough freshwater to raise sea levels worldwide by about 23 feet. Antarctica holds enough to raise sea levels by 215 feet.
- The Arctic Climate Impact Assessment projects that at least half of the Arctic's summer sea ice will melt by the end of the century.

Facts About Hurricanes

- According to Kevin Trenberth and Dennis Shea of the National Center for Atmospheric Research, global warming was responsible for about half of the increase in sea temperature in 2005 and that this increased warmth increased the intensity of that year's hurricanes.
- According to Christopher Landsea, a meteorologist at the Atlantic Oceanographic and Meteorological Laboratory, the current increase in hurricane activity is part of a natural cycle called the Atlantic multi-decadal mode.

Glossary

anthropogenic: Caused by human activity. Anthropogenic global warming is that portion of warming (if any) which results from human activities, especially the burning of fossil fuels.

carbon sequestration: An advanced technology that captures carbon dioxide before it enters the atmosphere and stores it underground.

carbon sink: A natural resource that absorbs more carbon than it releases. Rain forests are generally considered to be carbon sinks although new studies indicate that this might not be the case.

global dimming: The presence of carbon dioxide in clouds which deflects radiation from the sun, preventing it from reaching Earth. This is thought by many to reduce evaporation from lakes and oceans which in turn can lead to drought conditions.

greenhouse gases: Gases in Earth's atmosphere that trap radiation by reflecting it back to Earth. The major greenhouse gases are water vapor, carbon dioxide, and methane.

hydrological cycle: The movement of water from lakes and oceans to the air (via evaporation), to the land (via condensation in the form of rain and snow), and then back to the ocean as runoff.

ice core records: These are literally cores of ice, drilled as much as two miles deep, which are extracted and then analyzed to determine carbon dioxide levels. Because ice at these locations in Antarctica remains permanently frozen, the deeper ice represents earlier dates and the shallower ice represents more current times.

Kyoto Protocol: A treaty that went into effect in 2005. By this treaty, the ratifying countries have until 2012 to reduce their carbon dioxide emissions to specific levels below the 1990 benchmark levels.

Milankovitch cycles: Changes in the amount of solar radiation reaching Earth due to changes in Earth's orbit, rotation, and tilt on its axis. These are all natural factors that influence global temperatures.

multi-decadal cycle: A weather cycle that recurs over periods measured in decades rather than in years or smaller increments. Hurricane activity seems to recur in cycles of thirty-five to forty years.

natural variability: Changes that are not caused by human activity but that do inflict changes on Earth's climate. These could include such things as tides and changes in the jet stream air currents.

positive feedback loop: A cycle of events that continually increases the next event in the cycle. As an example, warming oceans could melt ice. With less ice, there is more open water which absorbs more sun than ice does. Absorbing more sun increases the temperature of the ocean which in turn melts more ice.

renewable energy: Energy forms that do not result in depletion of the energy-giving resources. Examples are wind power, solar power, and hydropower. Using these energy forms does not reduce the amount available.

tipping point: The point at which a projected change becomes unstoppable. Some people feel that once a certain amount of global warming occurs, it will be impossible to reverse.

tropical forests: Forests that grow in winter-free climates with high temperatures and high annual rainfall, including rain forests.

Climate Solutions
219 Legion Way, Suite 201
Olympia, WA 98501-1113
(360) 352-1763
e-mail: info@climatesolutions.org
Web site: http://climatesolutions.org
Climate Solutions' mission is to stop global warming at the earliest possible point by helping the northwest region of the United States to develop practical and profitable solutions.

Competitive Enterprise Institute (CEI)
1001 Connecticut Ave. NW, Suite 1250
Washington, DC 20036
(202) 331-1010
fax: (202) 331-0640
e-mail: info@cei.org
Web site: www.cei.org

CEI is a nonprofit organization dedicated to the principles of free enterprise and limited government. Rather than promoting government regulation, it advocates removing governmental barriers and using private incentives to protect the environment.

Cooler Heads Coalition
c/o Consumer Alert
1001 Connecticut Ave. NW, Suite 1128
Washington, DC 20036
(202)-467-5809
fax: (202) 467-5814
Web site: www.globalwarming.org

The Cooler Heads Coalition is a subgroup of the National Consumer Coalition and was founded by that group to debunk what they regard as myths of global warming. Features of the Web site include economic arguments against the Kyoto Protocol and other climate change policy documents as well as regular legislative updates.

Friends of the Earth
1717 Massachusetts Ave. NW
Washington, DC 20036
(877) 843-8687
fax: (202) 783-0444
e-mail: foe@foe.org
Web site: www.foe.org

Friends of the Earth is an activist organization dedicated to protecting the planet from environmental disaster. It has worked for renewable energy development, limitation of carbon dioxide emissions, and protection of the environment.

Global Warming International Center (GWIC)
PO Box 50303
Palo Alto, CA 94303
(630) 910-1551
fax: (630) 910-1561
Web site: www.globalwarming.net

GWIC is an international body that disseminates information on science and policy concerning global warming. It serves both governmental and nongovernmental organizations as well as industries in more than one hundred countries. The center sponsors unbiased research supporting the understanding of global warming.

Greenpeace USA
702 H St. NW, Suite 300
Washington, DC 20001
(202) 462-117
Web site: www.greenpeace.org/usa

Greenpeace has long campaigned against environmental degradation, urging government and industry to prevent climate change, protect forests, save the oceans, and stop nuclear threats. It uses controversial direct-action techniques and strives for media coverage of its actions in an effort to educate the public. Greenpeace publishes reports and pamphlets about climate and energy, forests, and genetic engineering of crops.

The Heartland Institute
19 South LaSalle St., Suite 903
Chicago, IL 60603
(312) 377-4000
Web site: www.heartland.org

The Heartland Institute is a national nonprofit research and education organization. Its stated mission is to discover and promote free-market solutions to social and economic problems, including market-based approaches to environmental protection.

The Intergovernmental Panel on Climate Change (IPCC)
c/o World Meteorological Organization
7 bis Ave. de la Paix, C.P. 2300
Geneva 2, Switzerland CH-1211
+ 41-22-730-8208
e-mail: Ipcc-Sec@wmo.int
Web site: www.ipcc.ch

Established in 1988, the IPCC's role is to assess the scientific, social, and economic information relevant for the understanding of the risk of human-induced climate change.

The George C. Marshall Institute
1625 K St. NW
Washington, DC 20006
(202) 296-9655
fax: (202) 296-9714
e-mail: info@marshall.org
Web site: www.marshall.org

The institute is a research group that provides scientific and technical advice and promotes scientific literacy on matters that have an impact on public policy. The institute's publications include the book *Shattered Consensus: The True State of Global Warming* and many studies, including "Natural Climate Variability" and "Climate Issues and Questions."

Oregon Institute of Science and Medicine
PO Box 1279
Cave Junction, OR 97523
(541) 592-4142
fax: (541) 592-2597
e-mail: info@oism.org
Web site: www.oism.org

The Oregon Institute of Science and Medicine is a small research institute founded in 1980 to conduct basic and applied research in subjects immediately applicable to improvements in human life. Their petition project claims that "global warming is a lie with no scientific basis whatsoever." It has concluded that increased levels of carbon dioxide have had no deleterious effects on weather.

The Pembina Institute for Appropriate Development
Box 7558
Drayton Valley, AB T7A 1S7, Canada
(780) 542-6272
fax: (780) 542-6464
Web site: www.pembina.org

The Pembina Institute is an independent, not-for-profit environmental policy research and education organization. Its major policy research and education programs are in the areas of sustainable energy, climate change, environmental governance, ecological fiscal reform, sustainability indicators, and the environmental impacts of the energy industry. The institute pioneers practical solutions to issues affecting human health and the environment across Canada. It publishes numerous papers and reports relating to climate change issues.

Sierra Club
85 Second St.
San Francisco, CA 94105
(415) 977-5500

fax: (415) 977-5799
e-mail: info@sierraclub.org
Web site: www.sierraclub.org

The Sierra Club is a grassroots organization that promotes the protection and conservation of natural resources. It publishes the bimonthly magazine *Sierra*, the monthly Sierra Club activist resource *The Planet*, and numerous books and pamphlets.

World Resources Institute
10 G St. NE, Suite 800
Washington, DC 20002
(202) 729-7600
fax: (202) 729-7610
e-mail: rspeight@wri.org
Web site: www.wri.org.

WRI conducts policy research on global resources and environmental conditions. It publishes books, reports, and papers; holds briefings, seminars, and conferences; and provides the print and broadcast media with new perspectives and background materials on environmental issues. The institute's books include *Climate Science 2005: Major New Discoveries*.

Worldwatch Institute
1776 Massachusetts Ave. NW
Washington, DC 20036
(202) 452-1999
fax: (202) 296-7365
Web site: www.worldwatch.org

Worldwatch is a research organization that analyzes and focuses attention on global problems, including environmental concerns such as global warming and the relationship between trade and the environment. It compiles the annual *State of the World* anthology and publishes the bimonthly magazine *World Watch* and the Worldwatch Paper series, which includes "Mainstreaming Renewable Energy in the 21st Century."

For Further Reading

Books

Athanasiou, Tom, and Paul Baer, *Dead Heat: Global Justice and Global Warming*. New York: Open Media/Seven Stories, 2002. An explanation of the causes of global warming and why governments have not acted to prevent it.

Bailey, Ronald, *Global Warming and Other Eco-Myths: How the Environmental Movement Uses False Science to Scare Us to Death*. Roseville, CA: Prima Lifestyles, 2002. An anthology of articles arguing that technology will solve the problems associated with global warming.

Flannery, Tim, *The Weather Makers: How Man Is Changing the Climate and What It Means for Life on Earth*. New York: Atlantic Monthly, 2005. Presents a history of climate change. Offers an action plan to reduce greenhouse gas emissions.

Gelbspan, Ross, *Boiling Point: How Politicians, Big Oil and Coal, Journalists and Activists Are Fueling the Climate Crisis—and What We Can Do to Avert Disaster*. New York: Basic Books, 2004. Argues that global warming is the most important problem facing the world today.

Gore, Al, *An Inconvenient Truth*. Emmaus, PA: Rodale, 2006. An introduction to global warming and a summary of the global warming crisis. This book was also the basis for a documentary movie.

Kister, Chad, *Arctic Melting: How Global Warming Is Destroying One of the World's Largest Wilderness Areas*. Monroe, ME: Common Courage, 2004. Documents the many problems caused by Arctic melting.

Kolbert, Elizabeth, *Field Notes from a Catastrophe*. London: Bloomsbury, 2006. A straightforward review of the scientific evidence for global warming.

Labohm, Hans, Simon Rozendaal, and Dick Thoenes, *Man-Made Global Warming: Unraveling a Dogma*. Brentwood, Essex, UK:

Multi-Science, 2004. Argues that global warming is not a man-made phenomenon.

Langholz, Jeffrey, and Kelly Turner, *You Can Prevent Global Warming and Save Money*. Kansas City, MO: Andrews McMeel, 2003. A book of tips for individuals on ways to prevent global warming.

Leroux, Marcel, *Global Warming: Myth or Reality? The Erring Ways of Climatology*. New York: Springer/Praxis, 2005. Challenges the concept of global warming and suggests alternative causes of climate change.

Maslin, Mark, *Global Warming: A Very Short Introduction*. New York: Oxford University Press, 2005. A review of the current thinking on global warming.

Michaels, Patrick, *Meltdown: The Predictable Distortion of Global Warming by Scientists, Politicians, and the Media*. Washington, DC: Cato Institute, 2004. An argument that global warming will not lead to crises.

Philander, S. George, *Is the Temperature Rising?* Princeton, NJ: Princeton University Press, 2000. Analyzes the problems caused by global warming.

Schneider, Stephen H., Armin Rosencranz, and John O. Niles, *Climate Change Policy: A Survey*. St. Louis, MO: Island, 2002. A compendium of writing by experts examining the policies of climate change, this book assumes that global warming is real and offers advice on how to deal with it.

Sweet, William, *Kicking the Carbon Habit: Global Warming and the Case for Renewable and Nuclear Energy*. New York: Columbia University Press, 2006. An argument for the use of wind farms and nuclear energy to combat global warming caused by the burning of coal, oil, and natural gas.

Victor, David G., *The Collapse of the Kyoto Protocol and the Struggle to Slow Global Warming*. Princeton, NJ: Princeton University Press, 2004. A scientific analysis of the problems with the 1997 Kyoto Treaty.

Weart, Spencer R., *The Discovery of Global Warming*. Cambridge, MA: Harvard University Press, 2004. A review of the problems faced by researchers investigating global warming.

Periodicals

Amos, Jonathan, "Climate Food Crisis 'to Deepen,'" *BBC News Science/Nature*, September 5, 2005.

Augusta (ME) Kennebec Journal, "We Need Wind Power to Fight Global Warming," June 12, 2006.

Bloom, Noah S., "It's Getting Hot in Here: Global Warming Hits the Hub," *Harvard Crimson*, June 7, 2006.

Bodansky, Daniel, "Global Warming: What to Do About the Changing Climate," *University of Georgia Research Magazine*, Fall 2005.

Breakthroughs, "How Vulnerable Are We to Climate Change?" Summer 2005.

Brown, Tanya, "Purdue Research Ties Ocean Temperatures to Hurricane Frequency," *Lafayette Journal & Courier*, May 31, 2006.

Business Week, "The Race Against Climate Change," December 12, 2005.

Corbella, Licia, "Let's Put a Freeze on Global Warming Hype," *Calgary Sun*, April 27, 2006.

Derewicz, Mark, "Feeling the Heat," University of North Carolina, Chapel Hill, *Endeavors Magazine*, May 23, 2006.

De Weese, Tom, "Global Warming: The Other Side of the Story," *Capitalism Magazine*, May 19, 2006.

Discover, "Hurricanes Intensify Global Warming Debate," January 2006.

Eilperin, Juliet, "World Temperatures Keep Rising with a Hot 2005," *Washington Post*, October 13, 2005.

Erickson, Jim, "Plan to Stop Warming: Scientist Says Tools Exist to Stabilize Greenhouse Gas," *Rocky Mountain News*, June 9, 2006.

Green Earth Journal, "More Hurricanes," April 18, 2006.

Hamilton, Joan C., "Danger Ahead," *Stanford Magazine*, September/October 2005.

Haranyi, David, "Chill Out over Global Warming," *Denver Post*, June 14, 2006.

Hertsgaard, Mark, "Nuclear Energy Can't Solve Global Warming," *San Francisco Chronicle*, August 7, 2005.

Hess, Glenn, "Biofuels Are Poised to Displace Oil," *Chemical & Engineering News*, June 13, 2006.

Hindu: India's National Newspaper, "Global Warming: Nuclear Power Gaining Acceptance," June 8, 2006.

Johnston, Ian, "Polar History Shows Melting Ice-Cap May Be a Natural Cycle," *Scotsman*, March 9, 2005.

Kluger, Jeffrey, "Is Global Warming Fueling Katrina?" *Time*, August 29, 2005.

Krauss, Clifford, Steven Lee Myers, Andrew C. Revkin, and Simon Romero, "As Polar Ice Turns to Water, Dreams of Treasure Abound," *New York Times*, October 10, 2005.

Kunzig, Robert, "Two-Degree Rise Drops Rice Yield by 10 Percent," *Discover*, January 2005.

Micallef, Charles, "Global Warming—Will Malta Vanish from the Face of the Earth?" *Sunday Times* (London), May 21, 2006.

Milius, Susan, "Pumped-Up Poison Ivy: Carbon Dioxide Boosts Plant's Size, Toxicity," *Science News*, June 3, 2006.

Monbiot, George, "A Few More Nukes!" *Los Angeles Times*, June 11, 2006.

NOAA Magazine, "NOAA Attributes Recent Increase in Hurricane Activity to Naturally Occurring Multi-decadal Climate Variability," November 29, 2005.

Roach, John, "Global Warming Is Rapidly Raising Sea Levels, Studies Warn," *National Geographic News*, March 23, 2006.

Schulte, Bret, "Temperature Rising," *USNews.com*, June 5, 2006.

Sterling, Bruce, "Can Technology Save the Planet?" *Sierra*, July/August 2005.

Townsend, Mark and Paul Harris, "Now the Pentagon Tells Bush: Climate Change Will Destroy Us," *Observer* (London), February 22, 2004.

Trenberth, Kevin, "Uncertainty in Hurricanes and Global Warming, *Science*, June 17, 2005.

Wagner, Tim, "Time Is Running Out for Action on Global Warming," *Salt Lake Tribune*, June 10, 2006.

Wexler, Mark, "Confronting a Global Crisis," *National Wildlife*, April/May 2005.

Wilson, Janet and Peter Nicholas, "Western Governors Take Aim at Global Warming," *Los Angeles Times*, June 12, 2006.

World Peace Herald, "Global Warming Affecting Alaska's Forests," May 30, 2006.

Wotherspoon, Sarah, "Warming to a Global Cause," *Herald Sun* (Melbourne), June 5, 2006.

Web Sites

CO₂ Science (www.co2science.org). A weekly online publication by the Center for the Study of Carbon Dioxide and Global Change. It includes commentary on new developments related to the ongoing rise in the air's carbon dioxide content.

E-Team (www.eteam.ncpa.org). The E-Team is the environmental arm of the National Center for Policy Analysis. Its Web site consists of articles that question the science and dispute the conclusions of those who advocate government action to combat global warming.

Natural Resources Defense Council (www.nrdc.org). This Web site, by one of the nation's largest environmental organizations, advocates action to stop global warming. It includes international news articles citing specific problems that it attributes to global warming.

Real Climate (www.realclimate.org). A Web site where climate scientists provide up-to-date commentary in response to news stories related to climate science.

Union of Concerned Scientists (www.ucsusa.org). Presents information on renewable energy, global warming, and other related topics, along with action plans to combat global warming.

World Climate Report (www.worldclimatereport.com). This Web site offers articles supporting the view that fear of global warming is based on faulty science and that "climate change is a largely overblown issue."

Index

agriculture. *See* food supply
alarmists, 24
Alaska, 17–18
Alley, Richard, 75
alternative energy sources
    are inadequate, 47–48
    are needed, 20–22, 36–37
Amazon jungle, 17
Andrew, Hurricane, 10, 12
animals, 16
Antarctica
    global warming and, 77–81
    is losing ice, 72, 74, 76
Arctic Ocean, 72, 74, 94

Bellamy, David, 38
Bindschandler, Robert, 72
Brown, Lester, 89, 90–92
Burnett, H. Sterling, 82
Bush, George W., 60
Byrnes, John, 56

carbon dioxide levels, 16
    are not a problem, 28
    are serious problem, 46–47
    in atmosphere, 84
    benefits of increased, 40–41,
        83–86
    industrialization caused rising,
        32–34
    nuclear power will lower,
        45–51
    con, 55–56

projected, 54
    reducing, 19–22, 36
Christy, John, 27
climate
    affect of Earth's tilt on, 42,
        43
    see also temperatures
climate science, 24–25, 27
Cooke, Charles C.W., 12, 65
coral reefs, 19

Davis, Curt, 79
disease, 28
Dowdeswell, Julian, 76
droughts, 16

Earth, affect of tilt of, 43
Emanuel, Kerry, 60, 62, 63,
    66–68, 70
energy consumption, 19–20, 36,
    48, 53, 55

fear, 24
fertilizer, 41, 83–86
fires, 17
flooding, 19, 35, 41–42, 73
flood protection, 36
food supply
    global warming will decrease,
        88–92
    global warming will increase,
        82–87
fossil fuels, 16

are not causing global warming, 39–40
reduced consumption of, 19–20, 36, 48, 53, 55
in sea waters, 19

Gelbspan, Ross, 66
glaciers, melting, 17–19, 71–76
global dimming, 16
global temperatures. *See* temperatures
global warming
   benefits to, 28, 40–41, 82–87
   facts about, 93–94
   food supply and, 82-87, 88–92
   humans are causing, 32–37
      con, 38–44
   impacts of, 35
   hurricane activity and, 10, 12–13, 59–64
      con, 65–70
   is serious problem, 15–22
      con, 23–31
   nuclear power will help reduce, 45–51
      con, 52–57
   reality of, 46
   sea levels are rising from, 16, 18–19, 35, 41–42, 71–76
   sea levels will be lowered by, 77–81
   solutions to, 19–22, 36–37
Gore, Al, 10–12
grain crops, 89–92
Gray, William, 12, 67
Great Barrier Reef, 19
greenhouse effect, 18

see also global warming
greenhouse gas emissions
   benefits of increased, 28, 40–41, 83–86
   facts about, 93–94
   increased, 32–34
   nuclear power will lower, 45–51
      con, 52–57
   projected, 54
   reducing, 19–22
   weather and, 16–17
Greenland, 72, 74–75, 76, 80, 94

health, impact of global warming on, 28, 30
Heard Island glaciers, 18
Holocene epoch, 33
human activity
   is causing global warming, 32–37
      con, 38–44
hurricane activity
   effect of global warming on, 10, 12–13
   facts about, 94
   global warming intensifies, 59–64
      con, 65–70
   historical, 68
Hurricane Andrew, 10, 12
Hurricane Katrina, 9–10, 12–13, 60, 66
Hurricane Rita, 60
hydrogen cells, 47–48

ice ages, 42
ice shelf, 17–19, 71–76

industrialization, 32–34
Inhofe, James M., 23
International Climate Change
  Task Force (ICCTF), 16

Jackson, Derrick Z., 12, 59

Katrina, Hurricane, 9–10, 12–13,
  60, 66
Kennedy, Robert F., Jr., 66
Kerr, Richard A., 71
King, David, 41
Kormendi, Alex, 12, 65
Krabill, William, 80
Kyoto Protocol, 19, 41, 93

Landsea, Christopher, 12, 69–70,
  94
Lovelock, James, 17, 48

malaria outbreaks, 28
Mayfield, Max, 64
McCredie, Robert, 32
Mendelsohn, Robert, 28, 30
Miami, 12, 69
Milankovitch cycles, 42, 43
Mittelstaedt, Martin, 88

natural disasters
  effect of global warming on,
    10, 12–13
  hurricanes, 9–13
    global warming does not
      intensify, 65–70
    global warming intensifies,
      59–64
  increases in, 17
natural gas, 20

New Orleans, damage to from
  Katrina, 9–10, 60
nuclear power, 21
  is safe and cheap, 48
  will help reduce global warm-
    ing, 45–51
    con, 52–57

oceans
  acidic, 19
  Arctic Ocean, 72, 74, 94
  rising, 18–19, 35, 41–42,
    71–76
Oppenheimer, Michael, 72

plants
  beneficial effects for, 40–41,
    83–86
  negative consequences for,
    88–92
polar ice caps
  facts about, 94
  melting, 17–19, 71–76
property damage, from hurricanes, 12, 69–70

rainfall, 83
rain forest depletion, 16, 17
Ramana, M.V., 52
Reilly, John, 28
Reiter, Paul, 28
renewable energy sources. See
  alternative energy sources
Rita, Hurricane, 60

scientific disagreement
  about global warming, 24–25,
    37

over reasons for hurricane
intensity, 59–70
sea levels
facts about, 94
global warming will lower,
77–81
global warming will raise,
71–76
rising, 16, 18–19, 35,
41–42
Shea, Dennis, 94
solar radiation, 16, 18

Takagi, Jinzaburo, 55
temperatures
affect of Earth's tilt on, 43
are naturally cyclical, 42
are not rising, 25–27
averages in, 34–35
facts about, 93
historical changes in, 29

projected, 34
rapid changes in, 17–19
rising global, 13, 16, 17
see also global warming
tipping points
avoiding, 19–22
in global warming, 16
Trenberth, Kevin, 94
tropical reefs, 19

water vapor, 42
Watt, James, 32
weather patterns
changes in, 16–17
see also temperatures
weather satellites, 25, 27
Wenban, David, 15
wildlife, 16
wind turbines, 22, 47
World Climate Report, 77
Wynn, Terry, 45

Picture Credits

Cover: Tony Craddoc/Photo Researchers, Inc.
AP/Wide World Photos, 9, 35
Aurora/Getty Images, 17
Daniel Joubert/Reuters/Landov, 50
© David R. Frazier/Photo Researchers, Inc., 26
Getty Images, 49, 58
© Karl-Josef Hildenbrand/epa/CORBIS, 90
Kyodo/Landov, 40
© Larry Downing/Reuters/CORBIS, 61
Maury Aaseng, 13, 18, 29, 34, 43, 54, 62, 68, 73, 75, 80, 84
NASA, 56
NASA/Goddard Space Flight Center Scientific Visualization Studio, 67
NASA/GSFC/LaRC/JPL, MISR Team, 79
National Oceanic and Atmospheric Administration/Ocean Explorer, 14
Photos.com, 21, 53, 91
Reuters/Horacio Cordoba/Landov, 20
© Roger Ressmeyer/CORBIS, 33
Rupak de Chowdhuri/Reuters/Landov, 30
Scientific Visualizations Studio/NASA GSFC, 75
Shannon Stapleton/Reuters/Landov, 11
U.S. Department of Agriculture/Agricultural Research Service, 85
U.S.G.S., 73 (all)

About the Editor

Dan Minkel and his wife Julie make their home in Fayetteville, Arkansas. They have four children: Mike, Justin, Jared, and Emily and one granddaughter: Camille. Dan has been a construction project manager for over thirty years. This is his first project for Greenhaven Press.